Spectacular
Showers

FOR

Brides, Babies,

AND Beyond

Spectacular Showers

FOR
Brides, Babies,
AND
Beyond

Madeline Barillo

Contemporary Books

Chicago   New York   San Francisco   Lisbon   London   Madrid   Mexico City
Milan   New Delhi   San Juan   Seoul   Singapore   Sydney   Toronto

Library of Congress Cataloging-in-Publication Data

Barillo, Madeline.
    Spectacular showers for brides, babies, and beyond / Madeline Barillo.
        p.   cm.
    Includes index.
    ISBN 0-7373-0594-0
    1. Showers (Parties).   I. Title.

GV1472.7.S5 B37   2002
793.2—dc21   2001047211

Contemporary Books

A Division of The **McGraw·Hill** *Companies*

1 2 3 4 5 6 7 8 9 0   AGM/AGM   0 9 8 7 6 5 4 3 2 1

ISBN 0-7373-0594-0

This book was set in Adobe Garamond
Printed and bound by Quebecor Martinsburg

Cover design by Laurie Young
Cover photograph copyright © Photodisc
Interior design by Scott Rattray

McGraw-Hill books are available at special quantity discounts to use as premiums and sales promotions, or for use in corporate training programs. For more information, please write to the Director of Special Sales, Professional Publishing, McGraw-Hill, Two Penn Plaza, New York, NY 10121-2298. Or contact your local bookstore.

This book is printed on acid-free paper.

In loving memory of Josephine Foresta, who always loved a good party

Contents

Preface

LEGEND HAS IT that the first shower was given for a Dutch bride with a broken heart. Her father had refused to give her a dowry because she intended to marry a poor miller. The lovers married despite the threat of poverty, and the groom's friends pitched in and showered the couple with gifts of household necessities for their new home. Thanks to the shower of support, the bride's heart was mended—and her cupboard was stocked. It's a story with a happy ending.

That generous practice of showering loved ones with gifts and support has for centuries been wedding tradition. Showers are all about happy beginnings. In a way, showers are the most social of social occasions because they unite friends, family members, and neighbors for the sole purpose of helping someone special make a new beginning or complete a rite of passage.

According to historians, the word *wed* actually refers to the custom of purchasing a wife—when marriage was less a romantic proposition than a financial arrangement. The *wed* was literally the items (goats, chickens, gold coins, property) that the groom offered the bride's father to buy her from her family. This tradition gradually evolved into the concept of a dowry in which a bride's parents offered money, land, or goods to the groom for marrying their daughter. The dowry was also an assurance the bride would not go hungry; she would enter into the marriage with basic household necessities.

Throughout the ages, the concept of a bridal shower has taken many forms. In some cultures, a barn raising was held in which the bride's and groom's friends and family helped build a homestead. The whole community got involved; women cooked and served food while the men cut down trees for lumber, cleared the land, or built a foundation for a house. In other societies, the bride's friends contributed a trousseau or household items for her hope chest (typically a keepsake pine or cedar chest to hold linens or clothing).

In colonial times, Americans held showers for young women preparing for marriage. Friends and neighbors gathered to help the young woman sew a wedding quilt for her new home. As the women sewed, they gave the bride-to-be advice on love and marriage and prepared her to assume her new role in society. When a woman was expecting a baby, women gathered at her home to help sew baby clothes and make diapers. Men gathered to build a crib or cradle.

Today, showers aren't just for brides and babies. And they're not just "hen parties" held by and for women. Increasingly, showers are held for anyone—male or female—who is changing a job, going off to college, recovering from a setback or misfortune, struggling through an illness, or celebrating the adoption of a longed-for child. Showers can help people celebrate good times—or triumph over hard times. Everyone who is celebrated at a shower is making a life transition or taking on a new role. That could mean becoming a bride, becoming a mother, battling an illness, or starting a new career.

Showers are essentially affirmations of love and life and social unity. No matter what the occasion, when we give a shower for a friend or relative, we are saying, "Welcome," "We love you," or "We are here for you." (And you thought it was just about blenders or baby clothes!)

Planning a Spectacular Shower

Planning a party is a personal affair. This book is intended to make the shower-planning process easier. Each of the shower themes in this book includes suggestions for gifts, favors, decorating ideas, and menus, but these ideas are meant to be tailored to your shower's particular needs. Mix and match them, or use them as a starting point. You'll also find resources for buying everything from live butterflies to set free at the shower (no kidding), to hula skirts, party hats, and edible place cards.

The ideas for this book come from people of all ages and backgrounds who, like me, love to give parties or attend them. You don't have to be a professional party planner or spend a fortune to plan an unforgettable shower. All the ideas and tips are for real people who don't have months to plan but want to pull off a fabulous party.

If you're planning a wedding shower, pick up a bridal magazine for inspiration, or go to bridal shows and stop at every booth to collect free information and discount coupons. If you're preparing for a baby shower, noodle around the baby section of the local department store and get ideas for the latest baby products. Purchase a child-care magazine to get ideas for decorating the party room with baby pictures or to find lists of the latest books on baby care the new mom might appreciate.

For more information, visit the local party store or library. Party shops are chock-full of favors, accessories, balloons, special cake pans, and decorations to make any party festive. Libraries offer shelves of books on related topics such as entertaining, cooking, wedding planning, and child care. Save time and legwork by doing research on the Internet. It's a free source of immediate information. Log on anytime of the day or night and surf the sites for baby and bridal products, recipes, entertaining, and floral design.

Use this guide to celebrate the people you love! And may you, too, be showered with love, health, and kindness.

Acknowledgments

SPECIAL THANKS TO Valerie Foster for her wonderful recipes and fun newspaper assignments over the years; my parents, Marie and Joe Barillo, for their constant support; my editor, Maria Magallanes, with whom I have had the great joy of working on four books; Debbie Edelman, Olga Calle, and LuAnn Terlizzi, who gave me the best showers a bride- or mother-to-be could ever have; and the friends and professional party planners who kindly contributed ideas and recipes for this book, including Paula Gambs, Lynn Dennis, Steve Freitag, Jack Garceau, Liz Pisaretz, Roxanne Vartulli, Roberta Sekas, Donna Rienzo, Laurel Petersen, Nancy Doyle, and Donna Flagg.

1

Planning the Shower

"Debbie got engaged! Let's have a shower!"

Planning a shower can be a piece of cake. Once you've chosen the guest of honor, the theme invariably follows—bridal, baby, or specialty shower. Then it's a matter of when, where, and whom to invite.

Showers are unabashedly about presents. Piles of them. Friends and relatives giving them, and happy honorees unwrapping them until they're knee-deep in paper and bows. The sheer excess of it all makes people giddy. At a shower, the gift parade takes center stage; it's like at a child's birthday party. The guest of honor isn't expected to put the gifts aside and open them privately later. The showeree is *encouraged* to tear into those presents.

Showers have changed a lot since the days when they were ladies-only affairs. If you're old enough to remember miniskirts or lava lamps, you've probably been to your share of ladies-only showers where pink sherbet punch was served and guests nibbled on chicken salad with green grape garnish. Gifts were piled into a wishing well or frilly umbrella, and paper wedding bells or baby bottles hung from the front door. Guests were expected to play silly shower games, or embarrassing games with sexual over-tones. My Aunt Louise used to roll her eyes and "harumph" with disgust when someone recorded the bride-to-be's innocent comments while open-ing gifts ("Oh, I really need that!") and turned them into lewd wedding-night quips.

Not a male was in sight at these occasions; showers were considered an exclusively female club, and the groom or father-to-be was expected to show up just in time to tote home the gifts.

All that's changed now (although some people actually look forward to the pink punch—I confess that I do). Today, showers are hosted for brides *and* grooms. Expectant mothers *and* fathers. (It's no secret: men like get-ting shower gifts too.) Gay and straight couples. Grandparents. Showers are given for friends in the throes of a life change, move, or illness. Showers have evolved into lifestyle parties. They honor anyone who could really use a show of support or a brand-new set of cooking pans.

If your best friend recently got divorced and lost everything in the set-tlement, help him start over with gifts to restock and surround him with loving circle of friends. In a sense, showers are a combination of support group and shopping spree, love and laughter, punch and presents.

Much of the traditional etiquette surrounding showers has evolved as well. While it was once considered inappropriate for the bride's mother or sister to give a shower for her, the protocol has loosened, and the bride's mother often cohosts or helps pay for the shower. Showers are held for peo-ple living together and for people marrying for the second, third, or fourth time.

Showers were once small affairs held at home. These days that's not always the case. Showers often take place at a country club, woman's club, church hall, restaurant, or convention center. And, the guest list often tops one hundred or more. Imagine how long it takes to open gifts from one hundred people. . . .

Getting Started

When planning a shower, think carefully about the people you're going to invite, where the party will be held, and how you will celebrate. What element do you want people to remember most? The food? The decor? The theme? The venue?

It isn't necessary to spend a lot or to rely on a professional party consultant to plan a memorable party. The essential elements of any successful party are good food, great company, and a comfy place to sit. The comfortable-seat proviso may seem silly, but remember that showers tend to attract young and old guests, and a huge chunk of the party is spent sitting while someone else opens presents, sometimes for hours. Kids tend

How can I host a shower on a modest budget—without scrimping or cutting corners?

It's not how much you spend that matters; it's how you spend it. Consider a time of day when guests will not expect a full meal; or limit the guest list to a small circle of friends, which makes for a more intimate party. Ordinarily, a brunch or afternoon tea is less costly than a buffet or sit-down dinner. Ask friends to bring salads, rolls, and side dishes, and make the entree yourself. Or you might consider an elegant afternoon tea, which requires only tea cakes, cookies or sandwiches, and hot tea and coffee. Schedule an evening shower for after dinner, when a candlelight buffet of desserts, coffee, and champagne punch would be lovely.

to squirm and the senior aunties won't enjoy wobbly folding chairs after a while.

Choosing a Theme

Themes give showers pizzazz and add a unifying element. For specific ideas, refer to this book's separate sections on bridal, baby, and specialty showers. A theme, such as Queen for a Day, can lend an overall concept and influence the choice of shower invitations, food, decor, favors, games, and gifts. Guests might wear crowns while learning to wave like the queen and eat trifle with silver spoons. Or the theme can be translated into a single element only. For example, guests at an ABC Shower bring gifts based on the alphabet letter they've been assigned. (A guest assigned the letter *B* might bring a blanket or bib.)

Before choosing a theme, find out the kinds of gifts the guest of honor really wants or needs. Think about the crowd you're inviting. Will these guests enjoy—or barely tolerate—a theme-related activity such as making a craft or sewing a quilt? Would they get a kick out of sampling unusual ethnic foods or being asked to make wedding veils out of toilet paper rolls? If the answer is no, take a more traditional approach.

To Surprise or Not to Surprise

Ponder long and hard whether the guest of honor will appreciate a surprise shower. Planning a surprise party for an expectant mother is a dicey proposition. She might go into labor early and miss the party altogether. For any shower, it can be difficult to devise a workable ruse to get the guest of honor there, especially if he or she travels for business or has an unpredictable schedule. Be considerate of dress code issues. You don't want to mortify the bride by letting her arrive at a swanky restaurant in a halter top and cutoffs after telling her you were going to a picnic.

The Venue

If you're tired of squeezing into Cousin Martha's den for family showers, or want a larger or more interesting venue, consider holding the shower at a romantic country inn, historic mansion, winery, museum, or restaurant.

To find an unusual site, contact the local visitors bureau, chamber of commerce, or convention center, or log onto the Internet. Call the local college, church hall, or woman's club to see if they provide space for parties.

Imagine holding a baby shower at a petting zoo, surrounded by adorable baby animals, or hosting a retiree shower at the racetrack or near the shark tank of the city aquarium. "Join us as Arthur takes the plunge into retirement," the invitations might read.

Exotic Venues for Showers

- Aboard a sailboat, yacht, ferry boat, or floating barge
- In a nature preserve
- Inside a fragrant greenhouse
- At a department store (after hours)
- In the atrium of a landmark office building
- In a barn or in a farm meadow or paddock
- At a botanical garden
- At a skating rink
- In an airplane hangar
- At a racetrack

Art galleries can provide a fascinating atmosphere for showers. Guests mingle while discussing the weird or wonderful works of art. Landmark buildings with winding staircases or stained glass windows can also provide grand backdrops for photographs.

Keep in mind that you may need a city permit to hold a shower at a beach or park. And be forewarned. When planning a shower in a tented site on the grounds of a home or club, you'll need to provide many extras. "Creating" a site from scratch means all the amenities must be brought in, including portable restrooms, heating, air conditioning, flooring, cooking and refrigeration facilities, tables and chairs, and more.

The Menu

Once you've chosen a shower date and time, the menu choices will tend to fall into place. That's because the time of day dictates the kind of meal or refreshments served. Generally, guests have a right to expect a full meal if the shower is scheduled during the hours typically associated with breakfast, lunch, or dinner. That makes sense, doesn't it? Especially if guests have traveled a long distance to the party and will be hungry!

What will you feed the revelers? Keep in mind that unless the guests are professional chefs or food critics, no one will really remember the food unless it is truly awful or there is not enough of it. This sobering fact of life applies to most parties, including birthdays, weddings, and funerals.

Yes, food is important, but don't agonize over it too much. Try to remember the last shower you went to. Can you even recall what was served? Like most people, you probably remember the squeaky rattle the expectant mother received, or the fact that a psychic entertained the guests.

Hosts who'd rather not stage an elaborate feast can schedule the shower for a time when guests won't expect one—midmorning, midafternoon, or after dinner. A midmorning brunch, afternoon tea party, or elegant late night dessert buffet are also easy and economical ways to entertain a crowd with style.

For a brunch, serve plenty of hot coffee, an easy to assemble egg strata or sliced baked ham, along with fresh-squeezed orange juice, fresh croissants, and sweet rolls or bagels with butter, and an assortment of jams.

An elegant Victorian tea party is staged with surprisingly little effort. Use grandma's china or scour flea markets or garage sales for vintage cups and saucers that can double as party favors. Orphaned teacups and saucers (sold in lots of one or two) are inexpensive because most people prefer to buy them in complete sets. Ask the florist to fill a pretty teapot with fresh flowers. Serve hot tea with lemon slices or cream, along with scones and whipped cream, jam, tea cakes, petit fours, and finger sandwiches. Lay the table with embroidered or lacy linens.

For a post-dinner shower with a dessert buffet, warn guests on the invitations that only desserts and beverages will be served. Order a themed cake for dessert (in the shape of baby booties or the bridegroom's beloved fishing tackle box) and serve an assortment of strawberries, mints, fruit tarts, miniature cheesecakes, and chocolate cake. Toast the guest of honor with champagne, and place plenty of flickering candles around the room for ambiance.

If there isn't room for everyone to sit at table and guests will be expected to balance their plates on their laps, don't serve any food that requires using a knife. This is why the word *shower* conjures up visions of chicken salad, pasta salad, potato salad, and tuna salad. These dishes are a snap to make ahead and easy to eat with just a fork.

The classic ladies luncheon shower traditionally includes fruit punch, iced tea, chicken salad, date nut bread, fresh rolls, and miniature cookies or bars. But who says shower fare must be traditional?

Consider a barbecue with pulled pork or beef brisket dripping with sauce. Serve omelets made to order on a hot plate. Have an ice-cream sundae party. Let guests make their own single-serving pizzas. Spread a buffet with various take-out foods from an ethnic restaurant.

Choose uncomplicated dishes that are easily made ahead and frozen in serving pieces that can go directly from the freezer to oven to table. Don't even think of making a recipe you've never tried before. And avoid fussy recipes that require time-consuming steps just prior to serving. Wouldn't you rather be having fun at the party with the rest of the folks?

Many showers are potluck affairs, with guests volunteering to bring a designated dish such as a main course, casserole, side dish, vegetable, dessert, salad, or appetizer. Many hands make light work and everyone feels they have contributed something.

It's thoughtful to include some low-fat, low-calorie, and vegetarian entrees or at least side dishes that could double as a meal. And always give guests the option of diet, caffeine-free, and nonalcoholic beverages.

If you serve hors d'oeuvres, figure on each guest nibbling at least five per hour. That means if there are twenty guests and hors d'oeuvres will be passed for an hour before dinner, you'll need more than a hundred of them. For variety, serve three dozen each of three varieties, such as pigs in a blanket, shrimp puffs, and spinach quiche squares.

Have drinks ready in a punch bowl or set up bar-style for guests to serve themselves as they arrive. People seem to loosen up and mingle more easily with a drink in their hand, whether it's a martini or ice water. To save time, preslice the cakes or arrange desserts on trays and cover them with plastic wrap until you're ready to serve.

A few weeks before the party, determine whether you'll have enough serving pieces, glassware, plates, linens, flatware, and pots for coffee or tea. Ask a friend to reserve a few shelves in his or her freezer or refrigerator, if necessary.

To Cater or Not to Cater

No law dictates that showers must include home-cooked meals made by the hostess or guests. The shower police won't come and haul you away if you hire a caterer. Hiring a caterer to do all or part of the food preparation and serving will make for a stress-free party, especially if it's a full-service caterer who arrives with the food, arranges it attractively, serves it, and magically cleans it all up.

Depending on your shower location choice, the caterer may be an on-site banquet manager or someone you've hired from the outside to provide

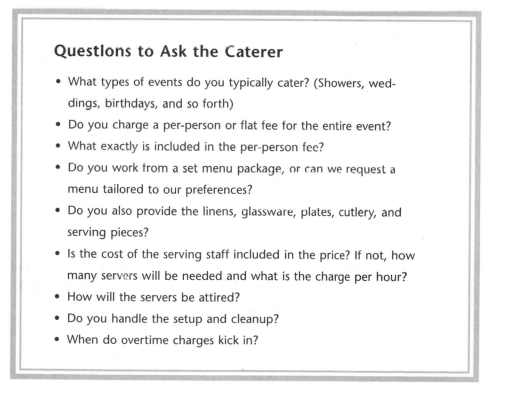

Questions to Ask the Caterer

- What types of events do you typically cater? (Showers, weddings, birthdays, and so forth)
- Do you charge a per-person or flat fee for the entire event?
- What exactly is included in the per-person fee?
- Do you work from a set menu package, or can we request a menu tailored to our preferences?
- Do you also provide the linens, glassware, plates, cutlery, and serving pieces?
- Is the cost of the serving staff included in the price? If not, how many servers will be needed and what is the charge per hour?
- How will the servers be attired?
- Do you handle the setup and cleanup?
- When do overtime charges kick in?

the food and beverages and sometimes the table linens, china, lighting, glassware, silverware, decorations, tables, and chairs.

Ask friends for referrals or ask your favorite restaurant if they offer banquet rooms for parties or off-premises catering. It's a good idea to comparison shop and meet with several caterers. Make an appointment to discuss menus, guest list size, and type of service (sit-down, butler-style, buffet).

Always sample the caterer's fare! You may need to schedule this for a time when the caterer is preparing food for another party, but it's crucial to ensure the food for the shower will be delicious and attractively presented. Nobody wants their shower to be the one where guests remember the meatballs with frozen centers or the tough-as-shoe-leather chicken cutlets.

A custom caterer is one who will work with you to tailor the shower menu specifically to your preferences. Other caterers offer set menus or packages that let you choose from a specified list of dishes, with few or no substitutions.

Never choose a caterer on cost alone. If the budget is limited, purchase prepared meals at a discount warehouse club, and make the salads and desserts yourself. Or hire a caterer to provide the main dishes and vegetables only, and ask guests to bring the fresh bread and side dishes.

The Guest List

When drawing up the guest list, keep in mind the amount of usable space at the venue. Look around the room(s). Is there ample space for food preparation, storage, and serving? Are there adequate restroom facilities? Where will gifts be displayed? Is there a cozy chair for the guest of honor to sit in while opening gifts? Will guests be able to see her or him unwrapping the presents? These details may sound obvious, but they are easily overlooked.

If the host has a studio apartment, it's probably wiser to host a small gathering of close friends rather than try to squeeze in dozens of people who'll be forced to impinge on one another's personal space.

Guests need a comfortable place to sit, room to move around easily, and a place to set their plates and glasses. Not everyone can handle balancing their fork, knife, and luncheon plate on their lap, so be sure to provide at least some tray tables or a place for some guests to sit at a table. It's especially important for shower guests to sit comfortably because opening gifts is the main act at a shower and it tends to take lots of time. Children and younger guests may enjoy sitting on the floor watching the gift parade, but older guests might find it impossible.

Don't assume a certain percentage of guests won't be able to attend. There's nothing worse than getting anxious every time another guest says yes because you didn't know where to cut the guest list!

Bridal Showers

Generally, it's thoughtful to include only those guests who are invited to the wedding, unless it's an office shower hosted by coworkers who don't expect a wedding invitation but want to celebrate the bride. In the case of a shower hosted by family or friends, most people limit the guest list to the female wedding attendants, the bride's closest friends and relatives, and possibly some friends from work.

If the party is for the bridegroom, ask the bride for a suggested list of friends, relatives, and coworkers. Conversely, if the shower is for the bride, ask the groom for a list of folks she'd want to include.

Some showers practically become conventions, with literally every female wedding guest invited, including people who have never laid eyes on the bride! Unfortunately, this practice makes the bride appear greedy and self-serving (even if the shower comes as a total surprise to her), and usually annoys guests who are forced to endure hours of gift opening.

There are no rigid rules about shower guest lists, but keep in mind that no one should be invited to a shower who is not also invited to the wedding. And certainly don't even think about inviting anyone who has never met the bride.

Baby Showers and Beyond

I remember attending a baby shower where the hostess invited some of her own friends—people the expectant mother had never met before. As this guest of honor opened gifts from total strangers, she kept looking up to scan the sea of faces, hoping to figure out which one was smiling most at her and perhaps guess whom to thank.

Be considerate. Don't invite anyone who has not personally met the guest of honor. Otherwise, it's awkward for both the person who is being showered and the unknown guest. Don't pad the guest list hoping to bring in more loot. Yes, it's nice for the guest of honor to get lots of gifts—but not from virtual strangers.

Inviting Children

Will children be invited to the shower? This is a thorny issue, because while showers are family-oriented affairs, it isn't fair to keep children up past their bedtime or expect them to sit quietly for an eternity while the guest of honor unwraps package after package.

On the other hand, some children love the pageantry and fun of a shower. Kids ten or older can be welcome little helpers. Assign them a task such as taking guests' coats to a designated closet or bedroom, bringing pieces of cake to guests, or handing gifts to the guest of honor to be opened. Children also can be marvelous at collecting the bows and discarded wrapping paper or passing trays of cold appetizers.

Invitations

A shower invitation tells the guest a lot about what to expect—how to dress, whether to expect a meal, and whether there is a theme or certain type of gift expected.

Showers are probably the only type of party where it's fine for the host to dictate the kinds of gifts expected or urge people to stick to a designated theme. If the party has a special theme, be sure to let people know on the invitation! If guests are assigned a particular type of gift, you must inform them ahead of time. ("Please bring a baby gift beginning with the letter *A*.")

Invitations should be sent at least four to six weeks in advance. Allow more lead time if the shower will be during the peak social season—from May to August—when guests often have competing obligations for weddings, graduations, and showers.

It's customary to send individual invitations to all guests sixteen or older, so if Gigi Brayboy and her sixteen-year-old daughter Maureen are invited, each gets a separate invitation, even if they live in the same household.

Generally, shower invitations are less formal than wedding invitations. Unless the guest of honor is royalty, skip the engraving, which is not only formal, but also very expensive. It's perfectly appropriate to purchase shower invitations or pretty note cards and write out the details by hand; or you can order custom-printed invitations from a mail-order catalog or stationery store. Making invitations yourself using a home computer is quick work these days, thanks to desktop publishing programs and a wide variety of papers, ribbons, inserts, vellum overlays, and envelopes available through craft stores and paper supply catalogs. Many catalogs will send free paper and ribbon samples. For more ideas, check out the invitation information listed in Appendix A.

Terms to Know

Engraving: A centuries-old printing process in which the text is cut (engraved) into the surface of a copper or brass plate. Ink is applied to the metal surface, which is then wiped clean, leaving ink inside the impressions. Paper is laid on the die, and a press forces the paper into the cavities of the die, creating a raised letter effect. Most people wouldn't consider engraving shower invitations; engraving is expensive and is best reserved for formal affairs.

Embossing: Embossing isn't technically a printing process, but it does press dimensional designs, text, borders, or artwork into the paper, creating a raised surface.

Thermography: In this heat process, wet ink and a resin powder are fused together on the paper to create a raised-lettering effect. Thermography is much less expensive than engraving, and most people can't tell the difference.

Laser printing: An inexpensive form of printing in which the ink lies flat on the paper. Best used for informal invitations.

Personal computer printing: Many home computers have software programs for printing informal invitations. Be sure to set the printer for the sharpest letter quality. Use high-quality paper stock or blank invitations available at stationery and office supply stores.

Calligraphy: An elegant form of script featuring flourishes and curls. The look can be achieved by computer (done at most stationery stores) or by hand.

Handwritten invitations: Purchase beautiful note cards or blank invitations at a stationery store and write them yourself using a fine-quality black pen that won't smudge.

If the guest of honor is registered at a store or online registry, include that information in the shower invitation. While it's never appropriate to list a registry on a wedding invitation, it's fine on a shower invitation.

Always order more invitations and envelopes than you expect to need. There may be last-minute invitees; it's also nice to have extras in case of goofs while addressing them.

Ideas for Unusual Invitations

Anything offbeat or three-dimensional catches people's attention immediately. Instead of flat cards, send a goodie in a box or tuck something unexpected into the invitation envelope. An invitation is more appealing if confetti or tiny candies spill out of it.

- For an afternoon Victorian tea shower, send tea bags tied with ribbons.

- Ask the baker to create wedding cake–shaped cookies and mail them to guests with the invitation printed on a recipe card.

- For a shower for a coworker, send invitations written on brown paper lunch bags.

- For a luau-themed shower, tuck a colorful *lei* or (silk) tropical flower into the envelope.

- For a kitchen shower, send a small cookie cutter with the invitation written on a recipe card.

- Write the invitation on a piece of antique-looking parchment. Include the message, "Royal Proclamation: Hear Ye! Hear Ye! A Shower Is Announced!" Tie this up with a ribbon and mail it in a cardboard tube mailer. (By the way, cardboard toilet paper rolls make handy mailers.)

- For a travel-themed shower, write the invitations on oversized luggage tags or paper airplanes. Or ask the local travel agent for airline ticket folders, and tuck the invitations inside the folders.

- If the guest of honor is a teacher, write the invitations on small chalkboards available at any office or craft store.

- Purchase blank, precut jigsaw puzzles at a hobby or stationery store. Write the invitations on the puzzle, then take it apart. Send the pieces sealed in an envelope for guests to assemble before reading.

- If the shower is for a reporter or some other kind of writer, print the invitations on spiral-bound notebooks.

- Is the honored guest a car enthusiast? Purchase tiny model cars and send each guest a car with the invitation written on the back of a map.

- For a baby shower, mail a rubber ducky to each guest with the pertinent date, time, and place written on a ribbon around its neck. Or write the invitation with a permanent marker on a disposable diaper.

- Print a baby shower invitation on pink or blue paper and tuck it into a plastic baby bottle or attach it to a baby rattle. Or purchase oversized paper dolls and write the invitation on the back.

- For a Chapeau Shower for a friend undergoing chemotherapy, buy doll-size straw hats or berets at a toy store and add them to the invitation envelope.

For inspiration, visit a party store, craft store, stationery shop, or office supply store, or go online. There are many websites devoted to products purchased by brides and expectants parents; most of them have sections devoted to shower ideas, menus, decorations, and entertainment.

Be sure to include the following basic information on the invitation:

• Shower theme

• Name of the guest of honor

• If it's a surprise (Be sure to let people know, and tell them exactly when the guest of honor will be arriving, so that they don't stray in late and ruin the surprise.)

• Date and time

• Venue

• Meal or refreshments (Give people an idea of what to expect, such as brunch, lunch, desserts and coffee, cocktails, afternoon tea, or dinner.)

• Name and address of host or hostess (If the shower is hosted by more than one person, don't forget to include all the names! And include the phone number of the venue, in case guests get lost on the way to the shower.)

• Guest of honor's favorite colors

• Guest of honor's decorating scheme

• Where guest of honor is registered (Include the phone number of the store.)

• Suggested attire

• Map and and/or directions (If the party will be in a restaurant or hotel, ask the banquet manager for preprinted directions. There's a pretty good chance the place will already have them. If you make your own, give accurate instructions with full street names and landmarks that will be easy for those unfamiliar with the area to recognize. Include exact distances from one turn to the next. Do a test run! Type up the directions and give them to someone who has never driven the route before. If the person gets lost, go back to the drawing board.)

Is it all right to send an invitation by E-mail?

If the shower is being pulled together on very short notice, and it's informal, yes. But otherwise it's preferable to mail the invitations or deliver them by hand. Here is a sample invitation:

Join us for a Travel Shower in honor of Christiana von Ritter
(Our favorite globetrotter is going to be a bride!)
Saturday, June 10
noon to 4 P.M.
at the home of her friend, Madeline Flagg
17 Waldron Avenue
Glen Rock, New Jersey 07452
Luncheon will be served.
Christiana is registered at Adventure Travels Ltd.
Her decorating scheme is peach and gold.
Travel-related gifts are suggested.
For directions and Regrets Only, call Madeline Flagg 712-334-1234.
Shhh! The shower is a surprise!

- Response information (Typically this is the last thing on the invitation. If the invitation includes the phrase "Regrets only," that means guests are not expected to respond unless they are unable to attend. The host assumes that anyone who hasn't called or written a note, is definitely coming. If "RSVP" is included, it means all invited guests are expected to notify the host whether or not they will attend.)

Planning Checklists

Professional party planners know that unforgettable parties don't just happen. The secret is to map out the little details beforehand so that on the day of the party, everything seems to fall magically into place; for example, the ice doesn't run out and no one arrives cranky because the directions were wrong. It isn't rocket science, just thinking each element through and visualizing the party logistics beforehand.

Take the time to write down your plans. A good place to start is by purchasing a loose-leaf notebook or folder with pockets to hold all the notes you'll gather or lists you'll invariably make. Or record all the shower plans on a home computer.

Then purchase a calendar and fill in the shower plans, week by week. Check off milestones as you complete them.

The ABCs: Absolute Basic Considerations

- Type of shower

- Guest of honor

- Hostess(es) or host(s)

- Shower theme

- Shower date and time

- Venue

- Approximate number of guests

- Budget

- Menu

    Beverages (soft drinks and alcoholic beverages)

    Punch, if desired

    Hors d'oeuvres

    Main course(s)

    Side dish(es)

    Vegetables, rolls, and butter

    Coffee and tea (decaf and regular)

    Dessert

- Favors (per guest or per couple)

- Is the shower a surprise?

Use the following checklist to determine what you'll need; whether you have to purchase, rent, or borrow items; and what you already have or what the caterer or party planner will supply.

Serving Pieces

- ☐ Bowls

- ☐ Platters

- ☐ Hot plates

- ☐ Coffeepot(s) for regular and decaf coffee

- ☐ Teapot(s)

- ☐ Sugar and creamer sets (you'll need more than one)

- ☐ Serving forks and spoons

- ☐ Breadbasket(s)

- ☐ Salad bowl

- ☐ Salt and pepper shakers

- ☐ Serving trays

- ☐ Doilies or tray decorations

- ☐ Cake or pie server

Tables and Linens

- ☐ Guest tables

- ☐ Buffet tables

- ☐ Tray tables

☐ Chairs

☐ Tablecloths

☐ Place mats for tray tables

☐ Napkins (cocktail, luncheon, dinner?)

Determine how many people can sit comfortably at each table, without feeling crowded. Don't rely on the caterer or banquet manager's insistence that "Of course ten people can be seated here!" Grab a bunch of friends and have them sit down and test it. When choosing tablecloths, think about whether you want the cloths to extend ten to twenty inches past the table surface, or drape to the floor; and whether you'll need additional skirting or overlays.

Table Size

☐ A 54-inch (square) card table seats four people.

☐ A 60-inch round table seats eight people.

☐ A 72-inch rectangular table seats six to eight.

☐ A 96-inch rectangular table accommodates up to ten.

Drinking and Dining Items

☐ Punch glasses

☐ Punch bowl

☐ Ladle

☐ Wineglasses

☐ Champagne glasses

☐ Beer glasses

☐ 12-ounce soft drink or iced tea glasses

☐ Coffee cups and saucers

☐ Teacups and saucers

☐ Coffeepot and teapot

☐ Plates: luncheon, dinner, dessert

☐ Flatware or silverware

☐ Water pitcher

☐ Cake knife

Flowers and Decorations

☐ Bridal wishing well

☐ Baby bassinet for gifts

☐ Floral centerpiece or other decorations for buffet table

☐ Guest table decoration

☐ Flowers for cake

☐ Floral bracelet or corsage for guest of honor

☐ Balloon centerpieces

☐ Helium balloons for archway

☐ Fabric swags

☐ Lighting

☐ Garlands, tent decorations, or pole covers

☐ Candles

Storage and Refrigeration Considerations

☐ Refrigerator

☐ Freezer

☐ Storage and food preparation space (You might want to ask neighbors to lend you space in their deep freeze or refrigerator; or arrange to store nonperishables in a home den.)

Don't Forget These!

☐ Extra trash bags

☐ Pencil and paper for recording gifts

☐ Tape for putting cards back on gifts after opened

☐ Camera, film, batteries

☐ Video or digital camera

☐ Enough ice

☐ Ice bucket or ice chest and tongs

☐ Enough glasses, dessert plates, forks, spoons (Remember that there may not be time to wash them between the meal and dessert.)

☐ Ample parking; "hidden" parking in the case of surprise shower

☐ Extra canvas bags, boxes, or shopping bags for bringing gifts home

- ☐ Accommodations for the disabled, or people with special dietary needs

- ☐ Props or items for shower games

- ☐ A place to hang or store guests' coats

- ☐ Plastic storage containers for leftovers

- ☐ Extra dish towels

- ☐ Guest towels for bathroom

- ☐ A quiet place for guests with babies to feed them or put them to sleep (Will they need a portable crib? Should they be reminded to bring one?)

Who Will Be Responsible For . . . ?

- ☐ Finding out the guest of honor's gift preferences and favorite colors or researching where registered

- ☐ Compiling the guest list and recording responses

- ☐ If it's a surprise shower, arranging the ruse to get the guest of honor there

- ☐ Recording gifts for the guest of honor (for writing future thank-you notes)

- ☐ Watching over gifts until it's time to open them (In a public place like a restaurant or hotel, it's not wise to leave gifts unattended.)

- ☐ Distributing favors (an ideal job for children or teenagers)

- ☐ Directing the party games

- ☐ Taking pictures at the shower or developing them for the guest of honor

- ☐ Transporting gifts back to the guest of honor's home (Is their car or van large enough?)

Planning Calendar

Party planning is all about details. The more planning you do ahead, the more fun you'll have at the party. Purchase an inexpensive calendar with big boxes for writing notes, or create one using a home computer. As each task is completed, check it off. Leave room somewhere for important telephone numbers (guests, caterer, florist, and so forth). It's handy to keep an over-sized envelope or folder with pockets for storing receipts, swatches, or deposit slips.

Two Months Before the Party

- ☐ Ask the guest of honor for their preferences of a date, time, or theme. (If it's a surprise, call their friends or relatives for input.)

- ☐ Set the date and time and choose a theme.

- ☐ Find out where the guest of honor is registered.

- ☐ Book a caterer or party site, if desired.

- ☐ Find out the guest of honor's color preferences, decorating scheme, and wish list.

Six Weeks Before the Party

- ☐ Prepare the guest list.

- ☐ Make or purchase the invitations.

- ☐ Prepare accurate directions to party.

Five Weeks Before the Party

☐ Mail the invitations and directions.

Four Weeks Before the Party

☐ Start recording acceptances and regrets.

☐ Plan the menu.

☐ Plan shower games and party favors, if desired.

☐ If using a caterer, or if the party will be in a restaurant, make an appointment for a taste test. Plan the complete menu with caterer or banquet manager.

Three Weeks Before the Party

☐ Determine if you need to borrow, rent, or purchase serving platters, chairs, tables, utensils, or linens.

☐ Purchase and wrap your shower gift.

☐ Calculate how much storage and refrigeration space you have and will need; make arrangements with a neighbor to reserve shelves in their freezer or fridge for you on the day of the shower.

Two Weeks Before the Party

☐ Make a shopping list of menu ingredients.

☐ Cook and freeze any dishes that can be made ahead.

☐ Determine which dishes will be served in which platters, and make sure that you have enough serving spoons and forks.

☐ Order flowers, if desired.

☐ Unless you are making it yourself, order the cake.

☐ Make or order shower decorations.

☐ Make a floor plan of the party. Where will guests be seated? Where will gifts be opened? Where will food and beverages be served? Where will guests park? Where will coats be stored?

☐ Purchase party supplies.

One Week Before Party

☐ Assemble the final guest count.

☐ Iron tablecloths and linens.

☐ If using a caterer or restaurant, provide management with the final guest count.

☐ Make calls to any outside vendors—florist, baker, caterer—to confirm delivery times.

One to Two Days Before Party

☐ Purchase groceries and prepare shower food.

☐ Put wine or champagne in refrigerator or cooler.

☐ Thaw any frozen main dishes or desserts.

☐ Tidy the house; clean the bathrooms.

☐ Decorate the house or shower venue.

☐ Pick up wishing well, or set aside place for gifts.

☐ Stock enough ice for drinks.

☐ Set up tables and chairs.

Day of Party

☐ Purchase fresh bread and rolls.

☐ Pick up flowers or cake.

☐ Prepare coffeepots in advance with water, filters, and coffee (but don't plug in until twenty minutes before the meal or refreshments are being served).

☐ Fill sugar bowls and creamers.

☐ Have a backup seating plan in case unexpected guests arrive.

☐ Have camera ready to take picture of the guest of honor arriving.

☐ Be ready one hour before the party, in case guests arrive early.

2

Bridal Showers

HERE'S TO THE BRIDE! A bridal shower is a joyous occasion. Surrounded by friends and relatives, the bride is the center of the universe for a few hours. She beams while unwrapping mountains of gifts.

Traditionally, bridal showers have been home- and hearth-centered. The brides invariably received kitchen and household staples intended to stock her cupboards and closets and keep her knee-deep in much-needed pots, blankets, egg timers, and rolling pins.

Most brides-to-be welcomed this largesse. Don't forget that less than two generations ago, most brides lived at home until their marriage. They established their married households from scratch. Setting up house was important. Few married women worked outside the home, and a woman's role was to create a loving, efficiently run household.

Today, most couples are two-career households, and modern conveniences have made running a home easier for both women and men. Kitchen showers are still as popular as ever, but special theme showers have also evolved that reflect a couple's shared lifestyle or interests such as gardening, cooking, sports, or travel. Why shower the bride with tea towels and canisters when she probably already bought them for her own apartment and would much prefer receiving a canoe or lumber to build herself a deck?

When choosing a theme, keep in the mind the bride's needs and interests. Will the shower be in honor of the bride, the groom, or both of them? Would the bride love a lingerie shower or quilting shower or positively hate them both? Will the party be a ladies-only affair, or will it include husbands, boyfriends, and kids?

Help guests be creative in choosing gifts by assigning them each a letter of the alphabet—or a letter from the bride's name and challenging them to bring a gift beginning with that letter (for instance, *C* for cookware or *W* for waffle iron).

Bridal showers are always more fun when guests do more than sip punch and watch the gifts being opened. Entertain your guests, treat them to beauty treatments, or lead them in craft-making sessions. Call the local music school and ask a violinist to perform. Hire an artisan to teach decoupage techniques, or invite a hairstylist or makeup/fashion color consultant to make everyone gorgeous.

Surprise shower guests by having them all meet at a spa or hair salon for a day of beauty during which they will be pampered with massages and manicures. Once everyone is relaxed and beautified, move the shower to the hostess's home to open gifts and have dessert. Or, invite a makeup artist to the shower and have everyone take turns getting made up while the gifts are being opened. Give guests bottles of nail polish or makeup brushes as favors.

Keep the party rolling by moving the party! Consider a progressive shower where guests gather for appetizers at one person's home, move on to another hostess's home for dinner, and then open the gifts and serve dessert at a third person's home.

For unusual favors, make miniature floral fortune bouquets. Cluster them in a glass bowl to use as a table centerpiece; give them to the bride to toss following the gift-opening. To make the favors, take three or four fresh flower stems per bouquet; wrap with florist's tape to secure as a bundle. Use a stickpin to attach a silly or serious fortune that's been printed or hand-written on a small strip of paper. Then cover the florist's tape with trailing silk ribbons, leaving the fortune exposed. The fortunes might include "You will be the next to marry," "How do I love thee?" or "Love is just around the corner."

For a new twist on place cards, write the guest's name on a piece of paper cut out to resemble a leaf or heart, and attach with ribbon to the stem of a piece of fresh fruit. Or use a hot glue gun to attach the name card to a tiny gourd or pumpkin or bride figurine from a craft store. Arrange place cards on tiny wooden chairs or music stands found in craft or party stores. Or write the guests' names on tiny strips of paper and glue to the shafts of little paper umbrellas (the kind that come in tropical drinks). Fill a shallow tray with sand and insert the umbrellas into the sand. For edible place cards, use pastry bag with a small round tip to pipe the name of each guest onto a frosted cupcake, graham cracker, chocolate fudge square, or chocolate mint cookie.

Household or Kitchen Shower

Welcome to the most traditional of all bridal showers. Gifts include kitchen basics, dish towels, spice racks, canisters, trivets, cookware, and so forth. This kind of party is sometimes called a "Miscellaneous Kitchen Shower" because guests are free to choose anything to stock the kitchen cupboards or counters.

Gift Ideas

Storage containers

Baking pans and pot holders

Cookware

Serving platters and utensils

Spice rack and spices

Coffee grinder and coffee beans

Electric can opener, coffeemaker, toaster, blender, or other small appliance

Microwave oven

Favors Wooden spoon with recipe card or refrigerator magnet

Decorations Borrow a toy kitchen set or child's plastic shopping cart from a friend with a young child. Pile the gifts around the little refrigerator or sink, or stack them in the shopping cart. Or purchase a dozen or more plastic pots and pans from a toy store, attach them to ribbons to hang from the ceiling. Make a centerpiece by filling a wicker basket or revolving lazy Susan with children's shopping cart groceries from a toy store.

Menu Create a festive spread of champagne or sherbet punch, crabmeat salad, fresh asparagus, a watermelon basket with fruit in season, and a lemon chiffon pie.

Lingerie Shower

Think pretty peignoir sets and lacy nightgowns. The lingerie shower is for the bride who may already have everything for the kitchen or would rather feel pampered in the bedroom. Gifts are anything the bride can sleep in or sleep on. They run the gamut from flannel nighties to furry slippers to sheets or lounging pajamas. For even more fun, invite guests to come to the shower in their pajamas and bathrobes.

The lingerie can be pretty, provocative, or practical, like woolen bed socks for cold winter nights. Just keep in mind that not every bride will appreciate peek-a-boo nighties or barely there thongs. College professor Laurel Peterson winces when remembering a surprise lingerie shower held in her honor. "Ah, showers. I hate them! I showed up to my own pastel extravaganza dressed in black suede, turquoise silk, and black lace stockings," she recalls. "My cousin, who was throwing the shower, had decided—without telling me—that I didn't have enough lingerie. So in this outfit, I spent the afternoon in front of my fiancé's business colleagues, and my very proper mother, opening packages containing filmy little outfits."

Gift Ideas

Nightgowns

Pajamas

Slippers

Bathrobe

Sheets

Decorative pillows and pillowcases

Bedside table lamp

Clip-on book light for reading at night

Silk stockings and garter belt

Teddy or baby doll pajamas

Bed socks or bed jacket

Gag Gift Flannel nightcap

Favors Night-lights or packets of hot cocoa mix

Decorations Create a dreamy bedtime atmosphere by dimming the lights and placing flickering candles everywhere. Have restful music playing in the background. As each guest arrives, hand her a mug of hot cocoa and a pair of cozy slippers to wear. Consider using a doll's bed for the table centerpiece, with the doll tucked in peacefully under the covers for the night. Write the invitations on paper dolls dressed in pajamas. Write "Sweet Dreams" on the place cards.

Menu Serve comfort food like Mom used to make: meatloaf, mashed potatoes and gravy, green bean casserole, and chocolate pudding.

Round-the-Clock Shower

On the invitation, guests are assigned an hour of the day (say, 7:00 A.M.) and challenged to bring a gift appropriate to that hour (an alarm clock or coffeemaker, for instance). Attach the invitations to toy watches or those digital plastic watches you can pick up for a couple of dollars at discount stores. Or cut out paper circles to resemble the face of a clock and draw in the numbers and minute/hour hands. Write the invitation on the back of the clock face. If there are twenty-four guests, each is assigned an hour. If not, double up the hours or stagger them.

Gift Ideas

7 A.M. Alarm clock

8 A.M. Coffee mug and coffee grinder

9 A.M. Commuter train ticket

Can the bride's mother host the bridal shower?

According to traditional etiquette, it's not appropriate for any immediate relative of the bride (mother, sisters, or future mother-in-law) to give the bride a shower. This is because it appears somewhat crass for anyone to request gifts for their own family member. Twenty years ago, it was unheard of for a close relative to issue the shower invitations. But in practice, however, it happens today, and the bride's mother might cohost the shower with the matron of honor or even pay the expenses for a shower officially hosted by the attendants, a relative, or family friend. No matter who plays host, the bride should never be asked to contribute to shower expenses.

When should the shower be held?

Bridal showers are generally held two to six weeks before the wedding, but there's no hard-and-fast rule. If the bride lives out of town, it may be necessary to schedule the party for when she is on hand for a dress fitting, or in the final days before the wedding. Likewise, if most of the guests will be in town briefly for the wedding, it may be necessary to squeeze in the party just prior to the wedding.

10 A.M. Memo pad for work

Noon Picnic hamper for lunch

2 P.M. Tickets to a matinee

4 P.M. Teatime basics such as teapot, tea bags, tea strainer

5 P.M. Cocktail shaker and barware, glasses

6 P.M. Items for cooking dinner

8 P.M. After-dinner board games or computer games

10 P.M. Bath salts, nightcap, blanket

Favors　To-do list pad or shopping list pad

Decorations　Borrow alarm clocks from all the guests and display them across the mantel or throughout the party room. Set them all to go off at the same time, perhaps when it's time to open the gifts or serve the dessert.

Menu　Set up three food stations and let guests choose their favorite meal time of the day. Prepare omelets and bacon at a breakfast time station, sandwiches and soups at a lunchtime station, and carved roast beef and gravy at dinnertime station. For dessert, set up a sweets buffet with cakes, pies, and cookies.

Holiday Shower

Does the bride or groom have a favorite holiday? Do they collect Christmas ornaments the whole year long or stockpile firecrackers in anticipation of a festive Fourth of July? Consider throwing a holiday-themed shower.

Popular holiday themes include Happy New Year's, Valentine's Day, Presidents' Day, April Fools' Day, May Day, Flag Day, Groundhog Day, Fourth of July, Halloween, Thanksgiving, Christmas, and Chanukah. But, you can always make up your own holiday to celebrate (Pie Lovers' Day) or log onto the Internet to look up obscure and dubious holidays listed on any of the electronic greeting card sites.

Gift Ideas

>   Christmas ornaments
>
>   Créche
>
>   Pinecone wreath
>
>   Christmas tree skirt, lights, and decorative candlesticks
>
>   Chanukah menorah and candles
>
>   Dredl
>
>   Heart-shaped Valentine baking pans
>
>   May Day flags and streamers for maypole dancing
>
>   American flag for Independence Day
>
>   Red, white, and blue place mats and star-motif plates and glasses
>
>   Firecrackers
>
>   Ceramic Halloween pumpkin
>
>   Halloween candy dish
>
>   Platters decorated with ghosts and goblins
>
>   Thanksgiving turkey platter
>
>   Turkey- or pilgrim-shaped Thanksgiving candles
>
>   Gift certificate for holiday brunch at a romantic restaurant

Favors Holiday ornament or calendar with all the major holidays circled

Decorations Decide if you're going the single holiday route or hosting a shower in celebration of all of them! If you're doing a Christmas

Shower in July, for instance, drag the Christmas tree and twinkling lights out of the attic and set them up in the party venue. Gifts might include holiday ornaments for the bride and groom, a tree skirt, holiday candlesticks, and Christmas-motif serving platters.

For a Halloween-theme shower, use a large pumpkin as the base for a festive table centerpiece. Trim off the stem end, then scoop out the soft flesh and seeds. Place some florist's foam or oasis in the bottom of the hollowed out gourd and fill with fresh chrysanthemums in gold, yellow, and rust. Add branches spray painted gold or black, autumn leaves, and sheaves of wheat. Serve hot cider, warm gingerbread cake with cinnamon-scented whipped cream, and candy apples. For favors, fill trick-or-treat bags with candy, or give guests masks decorated with feathers or faux gems.

If the party will pay homage to *all* the holidays, create decorated "vignettes" throughout the room. For instance, showcase Valentine's hearts and boxes of heart-shaped candy in one corner, Halloween pumpkins and masks in another, and Thanksgiving turkey and pilgrim figurines near the buffet table. Hang a large "Holiday Inn" sign over the front door for guests to see as they enter.

Menu Serve a meal consistent with the holiday you're celebrating. That means that if you throw a Thanksgiving Shower, for example, you serve a hot turkey dinner with cranberry sauce and all the trimmings—even in August!

Quilting Bee Shower

The hostess sends everyone a precut fabric square and asks them to decorate it any way they wish—with fabric paints, appliqués, sequins, buttons, or trims; or she can ask everyone to bring a square of fabric in a designated size, or recycle old clothes that have sentimental meaning into squares. They might bring a square cut from the bride's school uniform or favorite prom dress, or a square made from a loved one's blanket or clothing.

The guests can join in an old-fashioned quilting bee, just like in the days when neighbors feted the bride by helping her make a wedding quilt for her new home. If the group effort is too daunting, one talented sewer in the group can bundle all the pieces up when the shower is over and take them home to make a gift quilt on behalf of everyone. The quilt can then be displayed at the wedding.

Provide unusual entertainment at the shower by inviting a textile artist or accomplished quilt maker to teach everyone how to appliqué or make hand-sewn patchwork items to take home. Invite a member of the local historical society to bring antique quilts to the shower and discuss classic quilt patterns (Log Cabin, Wedding Ring) and how quilts and quilt-making once played such an important roles in the social and domestic lives of American women.

Gift Ideas

Quilted clothing

Quilted tea cozy or place mats

Quilt-making tools such as rotary cutter, templates, quilting needles, batting, thread, and fabric

Any gift made of fabric: tablecloths, curtains, pillows, apron, shower curtain, tote bag

Sewing notions: fabrics, trims, sewing kit items, quilting supplies, patterns

Gift certificate to fabric store

Gag Gifts Quilted toilet paper or paper towels.

Favors Purse-size scissors tied with ribbon or monogrammed handkerchiefs

Decorations Hang a colorful old quilt on the wall, and put grandma's lace doilies everywhere. For a tablecloth, use patchwork calico fabric or quilted bedspread.

Menu Serve an old-fashioned homespun menu of apple cider, chicken and dumplings, coleslaw, lima beans with bacon, warm rolls with butter, apple cobbler, and a rectangular sheet cake decorated to look like a quilt. In keeping with the neighborly theme, you might assign everyone a "potluck" dish to bring to the party. In that case, you yourself can simply provide appetizers, dessert, and coffee or tea.

Thanks-for-the-Memories Shower

Looking for a sentimental theme for an intimate shower? A Thanks-for-the-Memories Shower is a fun party for close friends and family of the bride. Everyone is asked to bring old photographs of the bride from her childhood and teenage years and write a poem or letter to her recalling the happy times they've spent together and good wishes for the future. As each guest shares their special memory, the letters and photographs are placed in a scrapbook for the bride to keep.

Have boxes of tissues on hand, this shower can get pretty emotional! But guests also share lots of laughs looking at the pictures, especially if most of them have known each other their whole lives and can relate to the people and places in all the pictures. The old photos of everyone in their toddler snowsuits will undoubtedly be hilarious.

Make a videotape of all the memory-making, and don't forget to record the stories of relatively new friends describing when and where they met the bride.

Gift Ideas

Family Bible, with page for family tree

Camera and film

Video camera

Scrapbook-making supplies such as archival paper and tape, stickers, acid-free mats, and borders

Family wedding veil to pass down

Ask the bride's family for old home movies to be made into a videotape

Make a donation to the bride's college scholarship fund or favorite charity

Silver picture frame

Pearl necklace

Antique earrings

Favors Give a special gift to the oldest and youngest guests at the party. Give every guest a pocket-size photo album.

Decorations Tape a six-foot piece of computer paper on the wall and create a time line of the bride's life, using scanned or photocopied pictures ("Here's Ann at age two in her party dress. Look at those frilly underpants!"). Have guests write in the exact month and year that they met the bride. Draw or photocopy a picture of a tree and ask relatives of both the bride and groom to write the members of their family tree, with birth and death dates and their relation to the bride or groom. The time line and family tree will be especially appreciated by the bride in years to come.

Menu Ask the guest of honor's mother for recipes for her favorite dishes from childhood, teenage years, college years, and young adulthood.

Paper or Lace Shower

Gifts for this shower are anything made of paper or lace—paper because it represents the first wedding anniversary gift (something to aim for) and lace because every bride deserves some. Gifts might be a lace mantilla for the bride to wear down the aisle or a framed and matted copy of the couple's wedding invitation.

Gift Ideas: Paper

Stationery

Books

Calendar

Fancy paper plates, cups, and napkins for entertaining

Paper picnic tablecloth

Accordion cookbook file

Photograph albums

Scrapbook-making paper and stickers

Gift Ideas: Lace

Lingerie or bedroom slippers trimmed with lace

Underwear

Tablecloths

Monogrammed handkerchiefs

Blouse

Favors Box of note cards

Decorations Visit a party store for inspiration. There are zillions of paper cutouts and decorations to choose from. Have photos of the bride and groom from their childhood through adult years scanned into a computer and made into a giant poster or photocopied for hanging on the walls. Or scan a photo onto a lace handkerchief to give the bride to wear as a corsage.

Menu Lay a festive table with gazpacho, cold shrimp salad, asparagus, spinach quiche squares, popovers, cantaloupe and blueberry salad, and butter cookies. Serve the meal as a buffet. Use decorative paper containers with metal handles similar to the ones takeout restaurants use. You can find solid color and printed varieties in specialty paper goods and party stores. Use coordinating paper napkins and tablecloths.

Victorian Tea Party Shower

Mind your manners, a Victorian Tea Party Shower is a civilized (and fun) way to celebrate a shower. Ask Texas resident Roxanne Vartuli. In honor of her future sister-in-law, she once hosted a Victorian Tea Party Bridal Shower in the conservatory of a local museum. Guests gathered to sip tea in china cups and nibble cookies, tea sandwiches, and trifle made from recipes from Buckingham Palace and the Savoy Hotel in London. The wedding party dressed in long white skirts, poufy lace blouses, and romantic hats. Each floral centerpiece was arranged with an antique teapot base. (The groom's mother had spent a year hunting down teapots at estate sales.) Each guest took home an antique cup and saucer as a party favor.

Gift Ideas

    Tea service

    Sugar bowl and creamer

    Tiered cake plates

    Silver teaspoons

    Pretty tablecloths and napkins

    Teapot

    Coffeepot

    Tea strainer

    Silver serving tray

    Book on afternoon tea etiquette

Favors Tea strainer or cellophane bags filled with exotic loose teas

Decorations Borrow or rent parasols. Fill clear glass canisters with penny candy for guests to nibble while the gifts are being opened. Lay the table with the laciest antique tablecloth and napkins you can find. Use a straw hat with plumes and a luxurious satin band as the centerpiece, or ask the florist to fill an antique teapot with fresh flowers. Break out the lace doilies and use them on chair arms or between the cups and saucers. Have classical music playing in the background.

Menu Serve hot tea, lemon slices, pitchers of cream, scones, watercress-and-cucumber finger sandwiches, tuna salad and crab salad sandwiches with the crusts trimmed, date nut bread, pound cake, petit fours, and meringues.

What kind of gifts are expected? At the last shower I attended, the bride received big, expensive gifts like computers and patio furniture! Whatever happened to toasters and electric can openers?

This is a personal decision, and if a guest wants to splurge on a blowout gift it's their choice to do so. But guests shouldn't feel pressured to spend a bundle, even if there's a troubling trend toward big-ticket presents. Remember, a shower gift ordinarily is not as lavish as a wedding gift. A considerate bride will register gift choices in a variety of price ranges. Guests can always take their clue from the theme of the shower ("Kitchen Gadgets Shower" or "Bed and Bath Shower"). If the bride demands only extravagant presents, she needs to learn a lesson in accepting modest gifts graciously. Or, you can split the cost of the item by giving a joint gift with other guests.

Can we list where the bride is registered on the shower invitation?

Absolutely! Gift registry information may be included on a shower invitation, but is never appropriate on a wedding invitation. However, it's considered crass to print a detailed gift list on the invitation. Just refer people to the place(s) she's registered.

Hold Everything Shower

Getting organized is quick work with shower gifts for creating order out of chaos. Choose gifts for organizing spaces in the kitchen, basement, garage, closets, desk drawers, or office.

Gift Ideas

Jewelry box

Hanging shoe organizer

Hope chest

Tie rack, belt hooks, lingerie drawer organizers

Kitchen storage containers

Quilted china covers (for storing place settings)

Segmented holiday ornament boxes

Accordion file for bills and receipts

Underbed storage boxes

Garment bags

Cedar chips and mothballs

Lint brush

Photo file boxes

Book on getting rid of clutter

Favors Coupon organizer file

Decorations Clip a magazine photo of a woman old enough to be the bride's mother, and draw in a cartoon "bubble" near her mouth with the words, "Mother always told you, there's a place for everything and everything in its place!"

Menu Have take-out food delivered; it will save time and prevent stress for the hostess.

Heirloom Recipe Shower

Guests bring their favorite family recipes to bind into a cookbook for the bride, along with a cooking or baking utensil needed to prepare it. For instance, bring Grandma's apple streusel pie recipe and a pie pan to make it in. By the end of the party, the bride will have a tried-and-true collection of everyone's favorite entrees, cookies, cakes, side dishes, soups, salads, and casseroles.

With the invitations, send each guest two recipe cards: one to write a recipe their mother handed down to them and the other to write down their own favorite. As each gift is opened, the recipe cards are inserted into a loose-leaf binder with plastic pocket pages for the bride to keep.

Gift Ideas

Cookbooks

Freezing and canning guide

Rolling pin

Pie plate

Jelly roll pan

Plastic cookbook holder

Sifter

Covered casserole dish

Favors Cheese grater

Decorations Give the bride an apron and chef's toque to wear as she opens the presents. Make her a "bouquet" from wooden spoons, whisks, and spatulas tied with trailing ribbons.

Menu Host a potluck luncheon with each guest preparing the recipe they're passing along to the bride. The hostess provides hot and cold beverages, salad, rolls and butter, and dessert.

Gadgets and Time-Savers Shower

Gifts are gadgets that make life easier! These can be anything from a combination kitchen pen and felt marker that attaches by magnet to the refrigerator or a hair-coloring comb with a built-in reservoir to distribute the color evenly.

Gift Ideas

Strawberry huller

Waffle iron

Bagel cutter

Egg separator

Corn-on-the-cob holders

Ravioli forms, pasta maker

Spaghetti measurer

Suction cup shelves for bathroom

Grip for opening cans

Apple corer and slicer

Towels with Velcro edges (for wrapping easily around wet hair)

Favors Egg separator or wire whisk

Menu Tomato and mozzarella salad with fresh basil, take-out pizza (save yourself some time!), hot garlic bread, and boutique beers. Serve a store-bought ice cream cake for dessert. Borrow or buy a cappuccino machine, and make frothy, steaming coffee drinks for guests to sip while the guest of honor opens gifts.

A Year's Worth of . . . Shower

This unusual theme is great for the couple just starting out or anyone who loves being prepared or hates to shop. Ask guests to bring a "year's worth" of anything for the household. The gifts needn't be extravagant, just as long as they come by the dozen or in an amount large enough to last one year. Useful items for this type of shower might include a year's worth of toothpaste, soap, shampoo, or paper towels, or a year's worth of spaghetti or pantyhose or lightbulbs or chocolate bars.

For group gifts, consider pooling resources for a "gift of the month" club that ships a different item every month of the year, such as a year's worth

The Bride's Tree Collection

According to an old German custom, the newlyweds' Christmas tree should include twelve symbolic ornaments to ensure health and happiness. These include a bird (joy), a teapot (hospitality), an angel (spirituality), a rose (passion), a fruit basket (generosity), a house (protection), a heart (love), a flower basket (good wishes), a Santa Claus (goodwill), a pinecone (fertility), a rabbit (hope) and a fish (God's blessing). These ornaments make wonderful favors for a holiday shower, or a thoughtful shower gift. All twelve ornaments in the "Bride's Tree Collection" are available in a gift set from the Signals Catalog. For ordering information, call 800-669-9696 or visit the Signals website at signals.com.

of flowering plants, fresh fruit, gourmet cakes, wine, scented candles, chocolates, or fragrant soaps. The Lillian Vernon mail-order catalog offers a gift box of twelve scented candles, one for each month of the year, and "A Fragrant Year" of twelve seasonal soaps from Scotland. For ordering information, call 800-545-5426 or log on to lillianvernon.com. Gardener's Eden, a mail-order catalog for plants, flowers, and gardening supplies, offers the "Flowering Bulb Series" of planted bulbs, delivered each month for a year. The blooms include pretty parrot tulips in April, amaryllis in December, and miniature iris in November. For ordering information, call 800-822-9600.

Gift Ideas

A one-year magazine subscription

Book-of-the-month club subscription

Annual membership in a health club

Annual membership in a warehouse buying club

A year's worth of video rental gift certificates

An annual subscription to the symphony

Manicures or salon treatments for a year

Lawn mowing for a year

A dozen dish towels for the kitchen

Gag Gifts A dozen donuts or a dozen eggs

Favors Pocket calendar

Menu Serve a buffet lunch or dinner with twelve platters: three appetizers, three entrees, three side dishes, and three desserts.

Made-It-Myself Shower

Hold the shower at a craft center or pottery making center and fete the bride while everyone learns to make something. A growing number of pottery shops offer instruction in painting or glazing ceramics. It isn't always necessary to start from scratch; many places have premade items to decorate. While the creations are drying or being fired in the kiln, guests have time to open gifts and toast the bride. Everyone gets to take home the vase, mug, or plate they made themselves. If you'd prefer a home-based party, invite an artisan, decorator, or craft specialist to come to the house to teach a skill like flower arranging, decoupage, stenciling, or painting on glass.

Gift Ideas

Craft supplies

Gift certificate to art shop or craft store

Paintbrushes

Pastels or watercolor paints

Sketchbook

Easel

Dozen wineglasses to hand paint

Favors Paintbrush or makeup brushes

Decorations Write the invitations on artist's palettes, made by cutting out a palette shape on heavy-duty construction paper. At the shower, display a large blank canvas or poster board on a large easel. Give guests paintbrushes and paints or colored markers and invite them to create a joint "masterpiece" for the bride. Have all the guests sign their names on the back. Who knows? It might end up displayed in the couple's living room.

Menu Create an artist's garret tableau by decorating a table with a red-and-white-checked tablecloth, wine bottles with candles, and posters of Paris. Serve loaves of crusty French bread, Brie, wine, croissants, and an assortment of cheeses and cold cuts. Make or purchase ladyfingers or cream puffs for dessert.

By-the-Book Shower

If the bride is a voracious reader or an aspiring writer, she'll love a book shower! You might assign each guest a category—cooking, travel, fiction, mystery, inspirational, decorating, crafts, how-to, reference, history, or biography—or give them the freedom to bring a blank journal book, inscribed book plates, scrapbook, photo album book, address book, or "book" of stamps.

If the bride is a student on a tight budget, she might appreciate textbooks and student notebooks. If she's a lawyer, consider law journals. If she's learning a foreign language such as Italian, order a subscription to an Italian magazine and give her an Italian dictionary. If she has a favorite author, call the writer's publisher and arrange for a book to be autographed.

Gift Ideas

Books of any category

Wedding-planning books

Cookbook holder

Scrapbook

Blank book

Bookplates

Reading lamp

Bookshelves or bookends

Address book

Page embosser with guest of honor's monogram

Favors Book of stamps

Decorations Decorate the party room with piles of books or books arranged by the yard with decorative bookends. Ask a baker to create a cake resembling a book. Place reading lamps around the room. For a tablecloth, use long sheets of wallpaper printed with a bookshelf background.

Menu Prepare dishes favored by famous authors such as Marcel Proust's beloved Madeleine sponge cakes; or re-create a meal served in a Charles Dickens novel or a picnic supper enjoyed by characters in a Jane Austen novel.

Queen-for-a-Day Shower

Treat the bride like a queen for a day with party fit for royalty. When the bride arrives, place a tiara or crown on her head, hand her a boxy pocket-book like the Queen of England carries, and place over her shoulder a royal sash made from white and blue satin and pinned with an oversized sparkly brooch. Address her as "Your Majesty!" and declare it her special day by reading from a royal proclamation you've made from a long piece of rolled-up computer paper or parchment. Throughout the party, refer to the groom as

Prince Charming and the bride's mother as the Queen Mother. Teach the bride how to wave to her subjects just like the queen, with a little tilt of the head and a twist of the wrist. Guests will be in stitches.

Gift Ideas

Queen-size sheets and comforter

Book on the British monarchy

Spa treatments, fragrant soaps, beauty items, spa slippers; gift certificates for manicure, pedicure, or massage

Pearl jewelry

Royal Velvet towels

Maid service for a week

A gift certificate for a ride in a horse-drawn carriage

A gift certificate for catered meals or the services of a professional chef

A night on the town in a chauffeur-driven limousine

Tickets to the Royal Ballet

A picnic hamper fitted with china plates, crystal glasses, and silverware

A wide-brimmed hat perfect for a royal garden party

Videotapes of royal-themed movies such as *Mary, Queen of Scots* or *Royal Wedding*

His-and-hers king and queen towels and pillows embroidered with crowns and the guest of honor's name.

Gag Gifts Anything "queen" size such as pantyhose

The maid of honor said the bride only wants deluxe yellow Egyptian cotton towels, and only from a certain bed and bath shop in town. What if I bring something that's not on the registry list?

Guests have the right to select their own gifts. While a registry certainly makes it easier to choose a gift, you aren't obligated to stick to the list. A gracious bride will say thank you for whatever gift you bring. If she doesn't receive every single item on her registry wish list, she can always purchase it herself.

What if the wedding is called off? Does the bride get to keep the shower gifts?

Generally, no. Both wedding and shower gifts are ordinarily returned to the giver when the wedding is called off. Which means the couple should refrain from using them before the wedding, even if it's tempting to do so. However, monogrammed items (like towels, sheets, napkins, and glassware) obviously are not returnable. There is no need for the bride or groom to bare their souls or go into personal reasons why the wedding is not taking place; a simple note saying the engagement has been broken is enough. If the person who gave the gift *insists* the bride or groom keep it, that's fine.

Favors Tiaras for everyone! Send guests home with gloves, old-fashioned costume jewelry, or a "royal" parchment scroll with a handwritten love poem or proclamation.

Decorations Hang up a royal proclamation that says, "I want no special treatment. Just treat me as you would the Queen." Have the bride sit in a "throne" decorated with velvet cushions.

Menu Serve Yorkshire pudding, roast beef, potatoes, or "bangers and mash" (British slang for sausages and mashed potatoes). For dessert, prepare traditional English fruitcake with fondant icing. Or serve a traditional English trifle made with sponge cake and gelatin or scones with jam, lemon curd, and Devonshire cream.

Psychic Shower

Invite a psychic medium, palm reader, or tarot card reader to give the bride and each guest a personal reading. It will be entertaining and people will eagerly line up to peer into the future.

Can't find a professional psychic? Have one of the bridesmaids dress up as a fortune-teller in a gypsy-style costume and make up silly fortunes for everyone. Before the shower, have the bridegroom inform her of things only he or the bride would know. The fake fortune-teller can then pretend to read the bride's palm and reveal such things as "You spilled orange juice on the kitchen counter this morning."

Keep it positive and lighthearted. The fortune-teller might say to the bride, "You are a very lucky woman! You will soon marry a wonderful man. I see you surrounded by people who love you. Expect many surprises and gifts today!" Set out a large bowl of fortune cookies for guests to nibble while the gifts are being opened.

Gift Ideas

Crystal ball, or anything made of crystal

Let's Take It on the Road

What to do when the bride, her parents, and her close friends all live in different parts of the country? Meet somewhere special. That's what friends of California bride Laura Gambs did when planning a shower in her honor.

Cohosts Marlene Pavelski of New Jersey and her daughter, Renee Pavelski of California, planned a wedding shower for Laura in Lake Forest, a suburb of Chicago. Marlene was able to do all the arrangements by phone and with the recommendations of friends who lived in Chicago.

Friends and relatives descended on the shower destination, the historic Deer Path Inn. They came from New Jersey, Michigan, Indiana, Wisconsin, North Dakota, Illinois, and California. Everybody traveled, and nobody minded.

"One of the best things about it for me was that it was a gathering of the women that I love, many of whom were at my wedding, and we had the next generation as the focus," recalled Paula Gambs, Laura's mother. "The support of all the grandmothers, mothers, and daughters was really magnificent. It actually felt like we were timeless, part of a clan that had been going on for a long time and now would be continuing on for a long time. On the surface, all the ladies were lovely and so were the flowers, games, and food. Below that surface was the feeling that women have probably had forever about support and love and nurturing the young and the old, too. It was great."

Good luck charms (four-leaf clover, rabbit's foot, or horseshoe)

Tarot cards

Ouija board game

Horoscope book

Cookbook for "cooking up" spells

Charm bracelet

Any gift for the couple's "future" together such as household items, furnishings, crystal, china, linens, small appliances, and so forth

Farmer's Almanac that predicts future weather

Perfume (labeled "Love Potion")

Candles and candlesticks

Gag Gifts Fortune cookies or daily horoscopes

Favors Tea leaves in clear glassine or cellophane bags tied with ribbon and a note saying, "Tea for sipping or fortune-telling"

Decorations Give the "psychic" a crystal ball to peer into. If you can't find one in a craft or costume shop, use an inverted glass fishbowl or glass terrarium bowl. Decorate the party room with twinkling lights or glowing candles, paisley tablecloths, or fringed gypsy-style shawls. For even spookier, horror-movie decor, hang garlands of garlic (to ward off vampires) and use dry ice to create a foggy, misty effect. To find a vendor that sells dry ice, just check the Yellow Pages.

Menu Serve a gypsy-style hearty goulash with rice. For dessert, bake cupcakes or cream puffs. Type out fortunes on small strips of paper. Laminate them with clear plastic, available at any office supply store. Then poke a hole in the bottom of the cream puff or cupcake and insert the fortune. Fortunes might include "The party will soon be over" or "Friends are a shower of love."

Around-the-World Shower

A travel-theme shower is most welcomed by the bride or groom who travels often for business or pleasure. The shower gifts are geared for making travel easier, such as travel-size toiletries, luggage, or gadgets. These items will come in handy for honeymoon travel, too. Write the invitations as an "itinerary," and ask your local travel agent for airline ticket folders to tuck them in for mailing. In keeping with the theme, use luggage tags as place cards, or write each guest's name on a tiny balsa wood airplane, available at craft and hobby stores.

Gift Ideas

Travel alarm clock, electrical adapter, travel hair dryer

Clothes that pack easily or need little or no ironing

Travel pillow

Cosmetic bags

Prepaid phone card

Travel coffeemaker

Assorted foreign coins and currency

Luggage or carry-on bag

Foreign language dictionary

Maps and guidebooks of honeymoon destination

Favors Leather luggage tags

Decorations Find out if the bride or groom has a favorite destination, such as the mountains or a foreign country they love to visit or have always dreamed of seeing. Call the country's consulate office for background information, or visit its website, and then devise games to test everyone's knowledge of the place. ("What export product is Costa Rica most famous for?" "How many pounds of grapes are crushed each year in the Burgundy region of France?") Ask a travel agent or foreign consulate office for travel posters, or decorate with maps and foreign flags.

Menu Choose an international-inspired theme such as a Mexican fiesta, Swedish smorgasbord, German Oktoberfest feast, or Italian pasta dinner. Look for menus and recipes in an international cookbook and decorate the table with appropriate-themed decorations such as castanets, sombreros, beer steins, or flags.

Wish-We-Could-Be-There Shower

Sometimes you'll want to throw a shower for a person who has moved across the country. All her old friends and family are here, but she's *there*. Don't let mere geography stop you!

You can hold the shower locally and leave an empty seat for the guest of honor or dress up a doll to stand in as her party proxy. Videotape all the action—from the first guests coming through the door to the dessert being served. Have the guest of honor's mother or a close friend open the gifts. Telephone the guest of honor during the party so that everyone can talk to her personally. Later, have someone pack up all the gifts and mail them to her.

Alternatively, send a party in a box! Arrange for all the gifts to be delivered on the same day and tell the couple to stay home that day and invite a few friends over. Explain to them that the shower is arriving on their doorstep. Arrange for a local caterer to deliver food, a florist to deliver flowers, and a baker to show up with a cake. Mail a party in a box with a disposable camera and prepaid developing mailer, hats, streamers, and decorations, along with a videotape with best wishes from all the people who have sent gifts. Call the bride-to-be at an appointed time while she opens the gifts.

Favors Postage stamps or scenic postcards

Decorations For a centerpiece, borrow two small dollhouses and connect them with a silk ribbon. Paint a corrugated box to look like a U.S. Postal Service mailbox and give each guest a stamped "Wish You Were Here!" postcard to write the guest of honor a note. Cut a hole in the mailbox for everyone to drop their letters into. After the party, empty the box and mail all the good wishes.

Menu Serve the guest of honor's favorite foods.

3

Showers for the Groom

MARRIAGE MAY BE A fifty-fifty partnership, but when it comes to parties for the engaged couple, the bride invariably hogs the spotlight.

In the past, the bride and her mother typically planned the wedding; the groom was merely counted on to show up on time. The bride was feted with showers, but the groom was counted on to show up afterward (which was just fine with some fellas). Though grooms were sometimes honored with a special groom's cake, they got the cold shoulder when it came to showers.

Today, more bridegrooms than ever are taking an active part in making wedding decisions—from the choice of the favors to the cut of the tuxedo— and showers exclusively for the groom are becoming commonplace.

At a groom's shower, it's the husband-to-be who sits surrounded by guests and opens package after package. The bride may or may not be included.

When planning a theme, keep in mind the groom's interests and the couple's shared lifestyle. Does he have a passionate hobby such as golf or skiing? Does he collect postage stamps or antique beer steins? Is he an aspiring chef who would appreciate gourmet cookware?

Don't feel compelled to choose stereotypical "guy" gifts such as power tools or sporting equipment. If the groom would appreciate new fingertip towels for the bath, buy them. If he and the bride *really* need kitchen basics, help them out.

Bachelor Shower

Don't panic. While bachelor parties tend to be known for wild carousing with the groom's best buddies and visits to strip clubs or screenings of adult movies, bachelor showers are generally tame affairs. Think of all the traditional elements showered on the bride—presents, punch, party games—and do it for the groom.

The guest list might include the groom and his male friends, best man, and ushers; or it may be a coed affair. Gifts can be anything you think the groom would enjoy—from computer software to china settings. Don't feel awkward about giving traditional household gifts to the bridegroom—just as you would the bride. After all, they will both need and use them. For a comical touch, use a frilly wishing well for the gifts, just as you would for the traditional bridal shower. And make sure the punch is pink.

Gift Ideas

Kitchen appliances, utensils, and gadgets

Wedding-planning books or magazines geared toward the groom

Humorous book on how to make women happy

Bed and bath items such as linens, towels, blankets

Gifts for entertaining

Barware and glasses

Stereo equipment

CDs and videos

Tools

Grill and grilling utensils

Deck and patio gifts

Home repair manual

Favors Pocket-size screwdrivers or miniature tool kits

Decorations If the groom has a sense of humor, decorate the room with the most traditional ladies shower elements such as doilies, flowers, and wedding-bell decorations.

Menu Serve chilled wine and beer, grilled steaks, potato salad, green salad with bleu cheese dressing, and triple-decker chocolate cake.

Hobby Shower

What's the groom's first love (beside the bride)? Is it building furniture? Collecting first editions? Cooking Indian cuisine? Shower him with gifts related to his hobby; or ask guests to contribute to a joint gift such as a season pass to his favorite baseball team's games or a workbench full of power tools.

Gift Ideas

Sporting equipment (in-line skates, bike accessories, cross-country skis, fishing pole, and wader boots)

Computer software

Cookware

Furniture refinishing supplies

CDs and videos

Flying lessons

Cell phone

Favors Playing cards

Decorations Tie the invitations and decorations to the theme. For a shower in honor of a sailor, purchase inexpensive wooden boats at a toy store or party store and write the invitation on the hull or sails. Decorate the buffet table with crossed oars and nautical caps.

Menu Serve a buffet with choice of several hearty soups, garlic bread, and salad. For dessert, offer trays of brownies and oatmeal cookies.

Stock-the-Bar Shower

For this party, guests are asked to bring all the items needed to stock a bar, such as glassware, utensils, or wines, beers, and liquors. Invite a professional bartender to demonstrate mixology techniques and teach guests how to make cocktails with unusual names like Fuzzy Navel or Chauvinette.

Gift Ideas

Old-fashioned glasses

Beer glasses

Champagne glasses

Ice bucket

Ice tongs

Corkscrew

Ice chest

Wine decanter

Mixology guide

Measuring cups

Martini glasses

Cocktail shaker

Cocktail napkins

Favors Decorative wine stopper

Decorations Ask a local liquor store for product posters or life-size cardboard displays.

Menu Put out bowls of pretzels, nuts, and other bar snacks. Serve grilled steaks or barbecued chicken with baked beans, corn on the cob, steamed broccoli, and deviled eggs. For dessert, serve a streusel coffee cake.

This-Is-Your-Life Shower

This party theme is part testimonial dinner, part roast. The closest friends and family of the groom gather to reminisce about their childhoods or bachelor days together before they send him off to be wed.

Ask each guest to bring a picture of the groom that can be bound in a keepsake scrapbook. As gifts are opened, guests take turns telling stories about the groom—what they did as children or college roommates, where they met, or how they survived their most challenging or embarrassing experiences together.

Before the shower, the host or hostess prepares a "This Is Your Life" book detailing the groom's milestone experiences ("Fred, here you are as a newborn in the bassinet"). Invite a few unexpected guests from the groom's past. It could be a former teacher, an old girlfriend, or a school chum he's lost touch with. Arrange for these "mystery" guests to hide behind a curtain or door. As they offer the groom their advice for a long and happy marriage, challenge him to identify their voices.

Gift Ideas

Photo album

Camera

Patchwork quilt

Computer software

Decorations Write the title "This Is Your Life" on a large scrapbook for the host to display the photographs guests bring. Make photocopies of pictures of the groom's childhood and adolescence and hang them on the walls. Hang a dark sheet or curtain across a doorway to conceal mystery guests until they are revealed to the groom.

Menu Ask the groom's mother (or a close relative) for his favorite recipes from childhood and re-create them for the shower.

This-Old-House Shower

Roll up your sleeves, a This-Old-House shower is for couples who are renovating a home. Guests volunteer their services to help the couple build shelves or wallpaper, paint, or improve their home. The shower begins early in the day and includes a relaxing dinner served after all the hard work has been done. Invite a building expert or craftsman to teach everyone a skill such as laying tiles or installing molding. Then set the guests loose to work side by side.

Gift Ideas

Lumber

Landscaping materials

Paint and brushes

Ladder

Shelving

Home repair book

Gag Gift Paint-by-the-numbers set

Favors Painter's caps

Decorations Place new paintbrushes of assorted sizes, rulers, and paint-mixing sticks in a painter's bucket; fill in with greenery and fresh flowers and use as the centerpiece. Display flowering plants on the steps of a ladder. Write the invitations on the back of paint-strip samples or on the brims of inexpensive painter's caps.

Menu Order pizza and serve cold beer and soft drinks. Ask a local baker to create a cake in the shape of a house.

4

Couples Showers

Until recently, the concept of a wedding shower for *both* the bride- and groom-to-be was an utter novelty. Showers were bridal affairs, thank you very much—exclusive parties for women by women.

That sexist attitude has changed. After all, why should the bride get all the attention? Couples today share the day-to-day responsibilities of cooking, cleaning, and running a household; the shower gifts ultimately will be used by both of them.

A couples shower is a great celebration for those who have been married before, or for couples who have many friends in common. Invite a coed group of close pals and hold an intimate dinner party, buffet brunch, barbecue, or poolside picnic. Or take the whole crowd out bowling or to the movies and return to the host's home for dessert and the opening of the gifts.

Many couples showers are real family affairs and even include children—the couple's own from previous marriages and those belonging to the shower guests.

Jack-and-Jill Shower

The bride and groom are both guests of honor at a Jack-and-Jill Shower. Guests are the couple's closest friends and/or coworkers, and the invitations request that guests bring one joint gift for the couple or a gift each for the bride and the groom.

The bride and groom take turns opening their gifts in front of the guests. You might decorate two special armchairs as thrones. Gifts are generally household and kitchen items, but the host or hostess can suggest any gift category. For example, if you know the couple is secretly hankering for a big-ticket gift such as an entertainment center, wide-screen projection television, or digital video recorder, consider pooling resources and asking guests to contribute to a joint shower gift.

Gift Ideas

Small appliances such as toaster, blender, microwave, or electric frying pan

Kitchen gadgets and utensils

Bed and bath items

Deck and patio items

Bar utensils

China place settings

Crystal

Favors Bottles of sparkling water, in keeping with the shower's nursery rhyme theme. (You remember, "Jack and Jill went up the hill to fetch a pail of water.")

Decorations Look for invitations with nursery rhyme motifs, or copy illustrations from a children's nursery rhyme book. Decorate with children's fairy tale books and plastic beach buckets, or look for a Mother Goose plush toy, or boy and girl (Jack and Jill) dolls in a toy store to use as a table centerpiece.

Menu Think about serving children's favorites such as macaroni and cheese, hot dogs, peanut butter and jelly sandwiches, lasagna, fruit punch, and ice-cream cake or chocolate chip cookies for dessert.

That's Entertainment Shower

If the couple already has the household essentials, give them the gift of entertainment. Invite all the guests to the theater or movies for a show, then return to someone's home to open the entertainment-themed presents and enjoy a late supper or dessert.

Provide director's chairs for the bride and groom to sit in while opening gifts. Write the invitations on movie director–style slate boards, available at party stores, or use a home computer to create invitations resembling theater tickets ("Admit One to Becky and Angelo's That's Entertainment Shower").

Gifts Ideas

CDs or videos

Gift certificates for the movies, tucked into a package of microwave popcorn

Theater or symphony subscription

VCR or DVD player

Board games

Jigsaw puzzles

Playing cards

Crossword puzzle books and dictionary

Novels

Computer games or software

Sports equipment

Favors Packets of microwave popcorn

Decorations Hang up movie posters on the walls. These are available free from many movie theaters after a picture has had its run. Provide the bride with a movie star–style feather boa and the groom with a director's beret and megaphone.

Menu Serve take-out food from a Chinese restaurant, and give guests chopsticks; or just serve desserts and coffee.

Ice Cream Social Shower

Looking for an easy way to entertain a crowd with a minimum of preparation? Everybody loves ice cream, and no one will turn down an invitation to an Ice Cream Social Shower.

Schedule the party for after dinner, when guests won't expect a full meal, and note on the invitation that coffee and ice cream sundaes will be served. Set up a long buffet table and offer several kinds of ice cream, fresh fruit chunks, peeled bananas for banana splits, whipped cream, sprinkles, maraschino cherries, crushed chocolate cookies, and white chocolate chunks.

Don't forget toppings: hot fudge sauce, caramel sauce, pineapple sauce, marshmallow fluff, and strawberry sauce.

This is a festive celebration for couples with young children; the kids can tag along and have fun right along with the adults. Don't forget to serve plenty of ice water to slake guests' thirst from indulging in so many sweets.

Gift Ideas

Ice cream maker

Old-fashioned ice cream sundae dishes

Ice cream scoops

Bowls and spoons

Bottled gourmet sauces such as rum, butterscotch, hazelnut, hot fudge

Decorative tray

Gift certificate to local ice cream parlor

Small freezer

Ice chest

Favors Chocolate-covered spoons or cellophane bags filled with sprinkles or jimmies

Decorations Order straw boater hats and parasols from a party store or mail-order novelty supplier such as Oriental Trading (800-228-2269). Guests will feel like they're at a turn-of-the-century ice cream social.

Menu Stock up on as many ice cream flavors as your freezer will allow. To make serving even easier, prescoop the ice cream into balls and return to the freezer. Roll some ice cream balls in coconut or crushed cookies.

To keep the ice cream from melting too quickly while serving, place the containers in a clean, new window box filled with crushed ice. Or place them in plastic top hats or ice buckets filled with ice.

Room-by-Room Shower

Ask each guest to bring a gift for a particular room of the home, such as the kitchen, bedroom, bathroom, deck or patio, dining room, and living room. Place wrapped gifts in the appropriate room.

The party moves from room to room as the bride and groom open their gifts. The last room they end up in is the dining room—or wherever a meal or coffee and cake will be served.

Gift Ideas

For the bedroom: linens, blankets, electric blanket, lamp, throw rug, chest of drawers

For the kitchen: spice rack, canisters, can opener, toaster, cutlery, knife set

For the bathroom: towels, facecloths, bath sheet, tissue holder, decorative soaps, shower curtain

For the living room: decorative lamps, vase, bookends, candlesticks, coasters, picture frames

For the laundry room: wicker laundry basket, laundry bags, shelving, medicine cabinet, storage containers

For the den: small television, bookshelves, coffee table, framed print, magazine rack

Gag Gift Give the bride and groom a copy of Virginia Woolf's classic novel, *A Room of One's Own.*

Favors Coasters or decorative bottle stoppers

Decorations Borrow a dollhouse from a friend with young children and use it as the table centerpiece. Wrap the party favors in little boxes and place them in each room of the dollhouse. Guests will have fun peering into the house.

Menu For this shower celebrating hearth and home, serve an old-fashioned supper like Mom used to make: beef stroganoff, buttered noodles, glazed carrots, iceberg lettuce salad with croutons, and chocolate cake.

Calendar Shower

The point of this shower is to fill up the couple's calendar with gifts or social engagements appropriate to each month. Invite a dozen guests and assign each one a month of the year.

It's fun to open gifts chronologically, by month of the year. As each gift is opened, fill in the date or time on a calendar for the couple. The gift need not be expensive—it can be a simple invitation to socialize in the giver's home, a gift certificate for some form of entertainment, or a promise to meet them for lunch or for shopping. It's also fine to have more than twelve guests. Double up on the months. For invitations, draw a calendar on a sheet of paper and circle the shower date. Roll up the paper and mail in a cardboard tube decorated with stars or colorful confetti.

Gift Ideas

January: Gifts appropriate to January might include a gift certificate for ski-lift passes or ski rentals or gloves and scarves with an invitation to a skating party.

February: Treat the bride- and groom-to-be to dinner at a romantic restaurant for Valentine's Day.

March: "Join Jim and me for hot cocoa and marshmallow toasting by our fire on March 7."

April: "You are invited to the square dancing party hosted by the Newcomers Club on April 10."

May: "We've ordered tickets to the symphony for May. Let the box office know which date you prefer."

June: Gifts might include beach toys or a beach umbrella for a day at a lake or by the seashore.

July: Invite the newlyweds to a Fourth of July picnic, or give them red-white-and-blue linens and napkins for planning a party of their own.

August: Gifts might include grilling utensils or a chef's hat and apron, or invite the couple to a backyard barbecue.

September: Make a date to join them for a Labor Day party, or treat them to a weekend getaway.

October: Give the couple silly Halloween masks and costumes, or invite them to a pumpkin-carving party.

November: This chilly month is the perfect time for a Sunday brunch invitation.

December: Give the couple a gift certificate for purchasing holiday ornaments, or give them serving platters and holiday-themed linens, candlesticks, or serving ware for festive entertaining.

Favors Pocket calendars

Decorations Purchase a blotter-size desk calendar and display each month on the walls. Guests can fill in the dates with social engagements, or write personal messages to the couple on them. Also, ask guests to circle their own birthdays, anniversaries, and special dates and give it to the couple for use throughout the year

Menu Along with a buffet meal, consider serving a few items traditionally sold by the dozen, for example doughnuts, rolls, or eggs (make them deviled).

Honey-Do Shower

Ask guests to bring a gift that the bride or groom can hand over to the spouse-to-be with the request, "Honey do this . . . !" The gifts can range from the practical to the romantic.

Gift Ideas

Blankets and comforter ("Honey, do make the bed!)

Gourmet ingredients and a cookbook ("Honey, do make my favorite meal!")

Tickets to a show ("Honey, do take me out for a night on the town!")

Grass seed and gardening tools ("Honey, do work on the garden and lawn!)

Lumber and brackets ("Honey, do make me shelves for the kitchen!)

Rug shampooer ("Honey, do clean the rugs!")

Ice chest filled with boutique beers ("Honey, do bring me a beer!)

Massage oil or liniment ("Honey, do rub my sore back!")

Manicure utensils and nail polish ("Honey, do paint my toenails!")

Paint and wallpaper ("Honey, do help me decorate the living room and den!")

Bedside tray and pretty china ("Honey, do bring me breakfast in bed!")

Lingerie and fragrant candles or sex manual (Let the couple fill in the blanks—in private.)

Favors Give everyone a small bottle of honey, tied with a ribbon

Decorations Look for decorations with the theme of honeybees, such as yellow and black napkins and a floral centerpiece with bright yellow sunflowers. Look for plush bees in a toy store and arrange them next to a honey pot on the buffet table.

Menu Serve a honey-glazed ham, tossed green salad, julienned carrots, baked potatoes, and honeydew melon for dessert. ("Honey, do bring me some honeydew.")

Remarriage Shower

What do you give a couple that is merging two households and already has "everything"? Give them a shower! Remember, even if one or both of them has been married before, in most cases it's their first marriage to each other.

The chances are good that anyone marrying a second or more time already has complete sets of china and crystal and all the appliances and steak knives they'll ever need. But they will certainly appreciate new sheets, towels, table linens, and gifts for recreation or hobbies.

Gift Ideas

His-and-her towels

His-and-her pajamas

Sheets, pillowcases, blankets, and comforters

Donation to a scholarship fund or charity

Picnic hamper filled with china, a blanket, champagne, and glasses

Tickets to the opera and opera glasses

Gifts for entertaining: punch bowl, serving platters, crystal water pitcher

Favors Give each guest a champagne flute and split of champagne

Decorations Take a cue from the couple's interests or personal history. If they met on a date to the movies, decorate with movie memorabilia and serve popcorn. Do they love the opera or theater? Make a theatrical floral centerpiece with fresh flowers accented with feather plumes and masks decorated with glitter.

Menu Anything goes. If the couple has a sense of humor, serve twice-baked potatoes, double chocolate cake, or refried beans. After all, many things are better the second time around.

Sugar-and-Spice Shower

For this party, ask guests to bring gifts that will add spice to married life or make it sweeter. You'll be amazed how clever the guests can be! For spicing up life, they could bring anything from fresh ground spices for baking and cooking, to lingerie and fragrant incense for romantic encounters. For "sweetness," present the bride and groom with a box of chocolates or a scrapbook of their family pictures you've made yourself. They'll say, "Oh, how sweet of you!"

Gift Ideas: Sugar

Maple syrup

Fudge sauce and ice cream toppings

Gourmet chocolates

Crystal sugar bowl

Silver sugar tongs

Honey pot and bottles of gourmet honey

A dessert-of-the-month club subscription

Bottle of champagne

Family photo album

Book of love poems

Spiritual or inspirational book

Quilt

Picnic hamper

Gift Ideas: Spice

Lingerie

Sex manual such as *The Joy of Sex*

Massage oil, candles, incense, silk sheets

Chili peppers

Gift box of cooking and baking spices

Cookbook and spice grinder

Assortment of salsas, barbecue sauces, or gourmet condiments

Gift certificate to a romantic restaurant

Gift certificate for a weekend getaway

Favors Sugared Jordan almonds (sugar) tied up in tulle bundle; and/or cinnamon sticks tied with a ribbon (spice)

Decorations Ask your florist to create a sugar-and-spice-theme centerpiece with fresh flowers and greenery combined with cinnamon sticks, peppermint sticks, or lollipops.

Menu Spiced nuts, sweet cider punch, spicy chili, sweet and sour chicken, rice, bean salad with sweet red peppers, and Father Tony's Buttermilk-Glazed Carrot Cake (See page 190.)

Two-by-Two Shower

For this couples shower, guests bring gifts in twos (one each for the bride and groom) or gifts with his-and-her themes. Another variation is to shower the couple with gifts that are traditionally sold in pairs or two parts, such as bookends, candlesticks, salt and pepper shakers, sugar and creamer sets, socks, or gloves.

Gift Ideas

His-and-her towels

His-and-her coffee mugs

His-and-her holiday stockings

The Symbolic Meaning of Spices

Did you know that spices were once believed to ward off evil spirits on the wedding day? Couples carried spices in their pockets or tucked them into the bridal bouquet for luck. According to Penzeys Spices, a mail-order seasonings company with stores in Connecticut, Minnesota, Wisconsin, and Illinois, in times gone by, spices were often given as good luck charms to bridal couples. Penzeys offers several "Spicy Wedding" gift packages featuring salad dressing mixes and other items containing spices traditionally used as wedding charms. Among the spices included are whole nutmeg, rosemary leaves, and star anise. Why these? Europeans once believed that a marriage would remain sound as long as there was a "whole, sound nutmeg in the kitchen." Rosemary symbolizes remembrance and eternal love. In the Middle Ages, rosemary became the herb of lovers. A whole star anise, a spice with many points resembling a star, has long been given as a keepsake to bridal couples in China, where anise trees are indigenous. During processing, the points of the star are often broken. Giving couples a whole, unbroken star anise, signifies the tenacity of marriage and the spiritual unity of the couple. For more information on spices, call Penzeys Spices at 800-741-7787 or visit penzeys.com.

His-and-her matching bathrobes or pajamas

Monogrammed pillowcases with his monogram on one and hers on the other

Matching baseball caps

Bookends

Pair of candlesticks

Two bedside lamps

The couple's favorite book or video and its sequel

His-and-her engraved silver goblets

Favors Packages of Hostess Twinkies (They come in twos!)

Decorations Scout around toy shops for a wooden toy set depicting Noah's ark and the animals he gathered two by two. Noah and the critters will make a perfect centerpiece.

Menu Serve a choice of two appetizers, two entrees, two main courses, and two desserts.

Night-on-the-Town Shower

This is an especially thoughtful shower for the couple who are just starting out or can't afford to go out for romantic evenings at fancy nightspots. Treat them to an unforgettable night on the town or several events (for example, ballroom dancing lessons and makeovers) leading up to one special night.

Gift Ideas

Gift certificate for dinner at an elegant restaurant or supper club

Tickets to opera, ballet, theater, or rock concert

Ballroom dancing lessons

Coupon for a limousine and chauffeur

Bottle of champagne and ice bucket

Corsage and boutonniere

Day of beauty, with hair styling, massage, manicure, pedicure

Gift certificates to a clothing store and the services of a personal shopper to help them choose

Evening wear

Favors Splits of champagne

Decorations Have Cole Porter music playing in the background. Place gold and silver helium balloon bouquets at the front door and on the guest tables. Cover the serving table with a glittery silver lamé tablecloth, or scatter glittery confetti across the table. Place flickering candles everywhere.

Menu Champagne cocktails served in tall flute glasses, filet mignon, roasted garlic potatoes, stuffed zucchini, glazed carrots, and for dessert, chocolate mousse or cheesecake.

Self-Improvement Shower

A fabulous party theme for anyone who loves learning! Guests dream up ideas for lessons—or consultations with experts—on any topics they know the bride and groom have always wanted to learn.

If the couple is redecorating a house, chip in for a consultation with an interior designer, architect, or landscaper. Or treat them to lessons on refinishing furniture or making kitchen cabinets. Many of the home improvement stores nationwide offer free or inexpensive classes on basic home repairs and do-it-yourself projects and renovations. Call the local high school or community college for its continuing education catalog of classes on topics ranging from cooking and ballroom dancing to foreign languages, jewelry making, and computer repair.

Gift Ideas

Dance lessons

Cooking lessons

Scuba diving classes

Ski lessons

Health club or gym membership

Museum membership

Tickets to art history lectures or other learning series

Gift certificate for furniture-refinishing classes

Gift certificate for a continuing education program at local college or community center

Gift certificates for spa or hair salon makeovers

Gag Gift Box of hair color

Favors Paintbrush

Decorations Tape a blank canvas on the wall and give guests paints and brushes. Set them to work creating a keepsake painting for the bride and groom.

Menu Invite a local chef to teach an informal cooking class at the shower, then sit down with guests to enjoy the meal they've made.

Mortgage Shower

While gifts of money are considered crass in some cultures, in others money is regarded as an extremely thoughtful present; one that allows the bride and groom to reach a financial goal or purchase an item they would otherwise be unable to afford.

A mortgage shower is not for everyone. But consider this unusual celebration if you know the couple is struggling to save for a down payment on a house. If guests balk at being asked outright to contribute cash or checks, encourage them instead to bring a gift the couple could use in their new house.

Many banks now offer mortgage registries. As with any other type of bridal registry, the couple simply registers at the bank, which then sets up a specially designated account to which friends and family make deposits. An acknowledgment of the gift is sent to the bride and groom.

If there's no mortgage registry in your area, ask a bank to set up an account.

At a Mortgage Shower, the bride and groom need not reveal the monetary amounts of the gifts. They can simply open each card and say something like, "Thank you, Uncle Fred, for helping us get a step closer to our dream home." Encourage guests to bring a wishing-well item, a token gift such as dish towels or paintbrushes that can be opened and acknowledged along with each mortgage gift check.

Favors House key rings

Decorations Bake a gingerbread house, or build a toy house from wooden blocks or Lincoln Logs for use as a centerpiece. Decorate it with trees and bushes from a hobby or craft store.

Menu Ask the bride's and groom's mothers for their favorite "homemade" recipes and re-create them for the shower.

Are showers female-only parties?

While it may seem that way, showers today are thrown for men as well as women and are attended by both sexes. New dads, grooms, grandfathers, and anyone celebrating a special event will appreciate it! After all, showers are special parties, and everyone loves a party. Why should the ladies have all the fun?

I've been invited to four showers for the same bride. Am I expected to go to all of them? How many showers are too many?

It's an imposition to expect guests to attend multiple showers. It's also expensive. I met one woman who had been invited to eight showers for the same bride. Not surprisingly, she felt angry and abused. Ideally, a guest should not be expected to attend more than one shower for the bride or groom and may politely decline. ("Gee, I'm already invited to the shower for Sally being given by her Aunt Meg.") This isn't always the case, though, since the attendants are generally included on more than one guest list, and the bride's siblings or coworkers often end up going to several showers, too.

A thoughtful shower hostess will confer with the maid/matron of honor to inquire about whether anyone else is having a shower and find out which guests will be invited. Any person who is invited to more than one party should be informed by the hostess that a gift is not expected at each shower. If it makes you too uncomfortable to arrive empty-handed, consider giving a token present or a "joint" gift with another guest.

Is it tacky for someone to record gifts/givers during the shower?

No, it's perfectly acceptable—and necessary. During the commotion and excitement of opening gifts, it's easy for the guest(s) of honor to forget who has given them what. At a bridal shower, the maid of honor or a bridesmaid ordinarily records a short description of each gift as it is opened and the name of the giver ("pale blue embroidered tablecloth with eight matching napkins; from Aunt Karen Hart"). At any other kind of shower, just assign someone who is detail-oriented to the record keeping. This allows the guest of honor to write accurate thank-you notes later. If there are a very large number of guests and dozens of gifts to open, the designated helper may be called upon to unwrap the gifts and present them with the enclosure card to the guest of honor.

5

Baby Showers

❖

BABY SHOWERS TEND to bring out the nurturing instincts in people, even those who prefer pets or plants to little people. Where else does the guest of honor get to hold up teensy shoes and doll-size sweaters for the guests to admire? Something about seeing very small clothes makes grown-ups melt and coo.

Baby showers usually are held a few weeks before the baby's due date. Too close to the date means the guest of honor might unexpectedly go into labor and miss the party. Too early makes some families uncomfortable; they worry that if the pregnancy is problematic, it would be too painful for the parents to have baby paraphernalia around.

Sometimes the shower is given after the baby arrives. Mom and Baby both show up, and guests take turns cuddling the new arrival. When Donna Rienzo, a lawyer and college professor from New Jersey, adopted an eight-month-old girl from China, her family feted them both with a baby shower held at a cousin's home. While Rienzo opened gifts, her young daughter slumbered peacefully in the next room. Guests took turns tiptoeing into the bedroom to sneak peeks at her.

When planning a baby shower, think carefully about whether it will be a surprise. When a woman is in the last weeks of her pregnancy, she may not be feeling her best. It's natural to feel tired and uncomfortable. She may not appreciate walking into the den for a nap and having thirty guests jump out and yell, "Surprise!"

Before choosing a theme, find out what the new parents really want and need. If they have children, chances are they've already got a crib, changing table, and stroller or baby carriage. Find out where they are registered. Be creative! There's no law that says baby shower gifts must be clothes or stuffed toys. If you think the mom-to-be needs spa treatments or pampering more than fuzzy booties, go for it.

If the couple is clueless about baby care, organize guests to each demonstrate techniques for diapering or bathing an infant using a doll or someone's real baby. Most new parents leave the hospital absolutely terrified about caring for a newborn, even if they've been fortunate enough to have had lessons in how to bathe the baby. Unlike toasters and VCRs that come with operating instructions, babies are sent home from the hospital without any manuals.

Ask the mom-to-be if she'd like to receive clothes in graduated sizes. Guests tend to purchase items that the infant will wear immediately or a few months down the road. That means baby Billy looks like a fashion plate for four months, then suddenly has outgrown all the adorable outfits his mom got at the shower (which defeats the whole purpose).

The best baby shower gift I ever received was an oversized quilted tote bag. Since the design was a cheery paisley print rather than baby duckies or ABCs, it did service as a diaper bag in the early years and later graduated to use as a carry-on travel bag and slumber party bag. The baby for whom it was intended is now fifteen years old and toting the bag to summer camp.

To keep the party rolling, ask guests beforehand to bring baby pictures of themselves to the shower. Display the photos on the buffet table and have everyone guess who's who. Or hire a caricaturist to draw pictures of all the guests.

Find out if the mother intends to breast-feed the baby. If so, gifts might include nursing blouses and nightgowns with snaps and flaps for discreet feedings.

Remember, pregnant women should not drink alcohol. Be sure to warn the expectant mother if wine or spirits have been added to the punch. If you do serve liquor, also offer a nonalcoholic alternative.

If the guest of honor already has other young children, invite them to the shower and ask guests to bring a baby gift as well as a small token gift for the "big brother" or "big sister."

Traditional Baby Shower

Write the invitations on newborn-size diapers using a felt-tip pen, or make your own diaper invitations from pink or blue paper triangles, folded like a diaper and secured with a diaper pin.

As guests arrive, have them sign a blank guest book and write a few lines of advice for the expectant mother. Instead of name tags, make "hospital bracelets" for each guest with their name and birth date. Fill a baby carriage or bassinet with the shower gifts, and serve pastel sherbet punch (a baby shower standard!). Attach pink and blue balloons to the guest of honor's chair, and give her a corsage made from baby booties secured with a diaper pin.

Gift Ideas

Teddy bear or stuffed animal

Crib, sheets, and bumper pads

Receiving blankets

Footed sleepers

Newborn drawstring nightgown

Electronic baby monitor

Night-light

Decorative lamp

Diaper bag

Baby growth chart

Baby brush and comb set

Changing table and pad

Favors Oversized lollipop or small bottle of baby powder tied with a bow

Decorations Hang diaper pins and rattles from the ceiling using pastel ribbons. Purchase cloth diapers and dye them pink or blue to use as guest place mats. Visit a discount toy store for items that can double as centerpieces such as teddy bears, a toy doll carriage, a doll high chair, or a dollhouse; or fill a pretty wicker basket with toy blocks and small baby-care items: pacifier, rattle, baby lotion, baby powder, and shampoo.

Menu Serve dishes that are easy to make ahead such as lasagna or lemon chicken, along with pasta salad, fresh fruit, cookies, and iced tea or fruit punch.

Pamper-the-Parents Shower

The baby is the star of most showers, but a Pamper-the-Parents Shower refocuses the spotlight on the expectant mom and dad. It's a great party theme for anyone who already has baby bibs and clothes or will be feted at more than one baby shower. Gifts are anything to make the last month of pregnancy easier (the last four weeks seem to be endless), such as offers of prepared meals, help driving the mom to her doctor appointments, or gifts that the couple will enjoy together.

Gift Ideas

Movie tickets

Video rental coupons

Rental of a ninth-month "baby beeper" for the expectant mom to page the dad when she goes into labor

Gift certificates for take-out food

Parenting books

One month's worth of pickles and ice cream (or whatever else the pregnant woman craves)

Baby-sitting coupons entitling parents to a Saturday night out

A weekend getaway for the couple after the baby is born

A month's supply of diapers

Gift certificates for his-and-her haircuts or manicures

Favors Pink and blue bubble gum cigars

Decorations To baby them with special attention, bring pink and blue
    oversized baby bonnets for the mom and dad to wear.

Menu Chicken salad, rolls and butter, fresh fruit platter, date nut bread,
    and coffee and tea. For dessert, serve sherbet or chocolate mousse in
    cleaned-out baby food jars, with tiny pink and blue plastic spoons.
    Dress up the jars with baby-themed stickers or paint.

Adoption Shower

Adopting a baby or child can be a long process. Often, the new parents have
little advance warning that their bundle of joy is arriving. They may get a
phone call and suddenly find themselves hopping a plane for a trip across
the country or around the world to pick up their child on a moment's notice.

If the couple hasn't had time to equip a nursery (or child's room in the
case of an older arrival), plan a party that provides the basics. Greet the parents at the airport with a sign saying, "Welcome home, to the new family!"
Plan the actual party for a few days or weeks after their return.

The shower theme or gifts might incorporate ethnic traditions from the
child's native land. When Peter and Donna Flagg adopted the first of their
two daughters from China, guests gave them red baby outfits—a color traditionally associated with good fortune in China.

Gift Ideas
    Clothes

    Toys

    Nursery items

Baby snuggly carrier

Backpack carrier

Baby bedding items

Parenting books

First-aid kit

Guidebook on when to call a pediatrician

Gift certificate for a family portrait

Telephone book with names and numbers of other parents who have
    adopted and can offer advice and support

Favors Miniature splits of champagne

I'd like to host a shower for a couple who has just adopted a baby. They've kept In very close contact wlth the blologlcal mother, and she's practically part of the family. Should we invite her?

Probably not. Unless the adoptive parents and birth or surrogate mother have an unusually close relationship, this will only make the guests feel uncomfortable, and it may be more difficult for the birth or surrogate mother than she might anticipate. Showers are sentimental, emotional affairs. Besides, showers are a special rite of passage and bonding ritual for new parents. Let them have the spotlight. If they wish, they can celebrate later with the birth mom.

Decorations Display framed pictures of the couple beaming on the day they picked up their child.

Menu If the adopted child is from a foreign culture and the new parents want to celebrate that heritage, choose an appropriate menu such as a Chinese feast of stir-fried vegetables, dim sum, and fortune cookies.

Grandparents Shower

Guests bring gifts to help the new grandparents prepare for their wonderful new role. After her first grandchild was born, Lynn Dennis of Connecticut was feted by members of her church. Her son and daughter-in-law were expecting a child but they lived in Maine, while Lynn and her husband were in Connecticut—too far away for such a special occasion. The joyous news of baby Kendra Bellefleur's birth was shared by cell phone right from the delivery room.

The women at Lynn's church, knowing how Lynn yearned to see her grandchild, surprised her with a Grandma Shower. Lynn walked into a friend's home for a prayer meeting and was met with "Surprise!" In the dining room, hung a sign that said, "It's a Girl!" in pink foil letters. The table was adorned with a sumptuous cake, fresh fruit salad, nonalcoholic sparkling cider, and little porcelain angels. Gifts included things for Lynn and her husband to share with her precious grandchild: picture books, a devotional for young children, finger puppets, a picture frame, a baby lamb, a hair band, and cassettes of soft music.

Gift Ideas

Grandparent's brag book (photo album)

Cookie jar

Nursery rhyme or fairy tale books to read to baby

Rocking chair

A baby kit with diapers, formula, diaper ointment, hairbrush, and blanket for the grandparents to keep on hand for visits

Receiving blanket

Portable crib

Patchwork quilt

Portable stroller

High chair

Favors Miniature photo album

Decorations Use dolls and doll furniture to create a table centerpiece. Or fill a shallow tray with water and tint it blue with food coloring. Float rubber ducks in the water.

We'd like to have a shower for a friend who is a first-time grandmother, but we've never met her son or daughter-in-law and they live across the country. Should we invite them?

It's a nice touch to send them an invitation, but it isn't obligatory. After all, the shower is in honor of the new grandmother. Invite your friend and her circle of friends and relatives. At a Grandparents Shower, gifts generally include presents the grandma and grandpa can use while baby is visiting (high chair, travel crib), photo albums for keepsake pictures, or gifts for the baby. It's your choice.

Menu Place a cookie jar on the table and fill it with fresh-baked chocolate chip cookies.

Multiples Shower

This is one party where duplicate gifts are welcomed! A multiples shower is for the mom who learns she is having two or more babies. Imagine realizing you'll need all the basics in duplicate, triplicate, quadruplicate, or more! That's dozens of T-shirts, diapers, and pajamas daily.

This is a good opportunity for guests to pool their resources and order multiples of gifts at the same time; you may be able to get a discount on bulk purchases, which means that the new mom will have three *matching* car seats or one stroller that seats three.

If the expectant mother is confined to bed during the final months, have the party in her bedroom or hospital room. You may need to get permission from her doctor first. Instead of bringing the actual gifts, wrap up a picture of the gift in a box with the note, "This is waiting for you at home!" or "The stork is delivering this present on Tuesday."

Gift Ideas

Lots of diapers!

Annual membership to a wholesale buying club such as BJ's, Costco, or Sam's

Baby bottles and nipples by the box

Cases of baby wipes

Storage shelves or containers for organizing at home

A small freezer or refrigerator for bulk buying

Contributions to a scholarship fund

A washing machine and dryer (This will be a much appreciated group gift!)

Gag Gift Bottles of vitamins for the new mother or a cookbook on cooking for a crowd

Favors Humorous book with stress-reduction tips

Decorations Purchase one teddy bear for each of the babies expected. Dress each bear in a baby outfit and arrange them in a single line on the buffet table or in a high chair. After the party, the mom takes them home.

Menu Order a six-foot submarine sandwich from a local deli or caterer. Serve with potato chips, pasta salad, and macaroni salad. For dessert, order a cake in the shape of baby booties or a teddy bear.

What Every Parent Will Need—Diapers

Looking for a practical baby gift that's guaranteed to be used? Every baby needs diapers. Mountains of them. Pampers has come up with a clever idea—gift certificate packs for disposable diapers. Just log on to pampers.com, then choose how many months of diapers you want to give (a one-, three-, six-, or twelve-month supply). Pampers will send the gift packs to you, or directly to the parent. The packs are redeemable anywhere in the United States. They also include Fisher-Price toys and are delivered in a decorative box with a personalized card.

It-Takes-a-Village Shower

This type of shower is based upon the ancient African proverb, "It takes a village to raise a child." This means that children benefit from the love and combined wisdom of their extended family and the members of their community. For this shower, gifts comprise offers of services and guidance. That could mean anything from an offer to baby-sit at certain times of the week or to mow the lawn or do the grocery shopping. For parents short on time and deprived of sleep, these gestures are priceless.

Gift Ideas

Volunteer to cook a week's worth of meals for the couple and deliver them to their door.

Offer to baby-sit the baby, or take their older children out for ice cream.

Volunteer to learn infant CPR and first-aid techniques.

Promise to show up with a bucket and cleaning supplies and clean the new parents' house from top to bottom.

Arrange for diaper service or purchase environmentally friendly cloth diapers.

Arrange for maid service for two weeks.

Arrange for a baby nurse to help out during the first week the baby is home from the hospital.

Compile a list of all the drive-through restaurants, banks, and stores in town (essential information for new moms who can get errands done without dragging the baby out of the car).

Give the couple a rocking chair and show up frequently to rock the baby for them.

Favors Miniature globes

Decorations For a centerpiece, string a jump rope or ribbon across the buffet table and use it as a clothesline to hang up baby clothes.

Menu Host a potluck buffet, with every guest contributing a favorite dish to the party as well as a second dish for the expectant mother to take home and freeze for later.

Baby-Memory-Quilt Shower

Ask guests to bring an eight-inch square of fabric to the party, hand painted with fabric paint or left plain. The squares may be made from purchased fabric, or cut from their own child's outgrown baby clothes or blanket.

At the shower, the guests gather to sew the squares together for a keepsake quilt to present to the guest of honor. Or, you can hand the squares over to a talented seamstress who later sews it together in time for the baby's christening or arrival from the hospital. Consider scanning family photos onto the fabric squares. For how-to tips, visit your local computer store or a craft or fabric center. The memory quilt might incorporate photographs of all the members of the baby's family, from great-grandparents to parents and siblings.

Gift Ideas

Sewing kit

Quilted clothing for the baby or mom

Quilted baby comforter

Quilt-making tools such as rotary cutter, templates, quilting needles, batting, thread, and fabric

Storage containers for craft items

Favors Travel-size sewing kit

Decorations Use an old patchwork quilt for a tablecloth, or hang one from the wall. Ask a florist to fill a sewing basket with fresh greens and flowers.

Menu Ask a local baker to tint loaves of bread pink and blue. Serve casserole favorites such as macaroni and cheese, tuna noodle casserole, beef stew, or chicken cacciatore and rice, along with corn bread and baked beans. For dessert, serve an angel food cake with fresh strawberries and whipped cream.

Good-Old-Dad Shower

Celebrate "Father's Day" a little early with a party in honor of the daddy-to-be. Invite just his guy friends or make it a coed affair. As guests arrive, give each one a bubble gum cigar wrapped with a pink or blue cigar label proclaiming "Welcome to John's Shower." Write guests' names on paper dolls to use as name tags or place cards.

Gift Ideas

Humorous books geared toward expectant fathers

Baby name book

Box of cigars

Book on where babies come from

Bottle of champagne

Baby bottles with instructions for "late-night feedings"

Phone tree with names and phone numbers of everyone who wants to be called when baby arrives

Favors Real or bubble gum cigars

Decorations Hang a "Father's Day" sign over the front door.

Menu Make an informal meal of hot soup or chili and sandwiches, along with platters of cheese, crackers, and celery and carrot slices with ranch dressing dip. For dessert, make trays of cookie bars and brownies.

Heirloom Shower

Observe an old family tradition, or start new ones. At an heirloom baby shower, guests bring gifts of old family heirlooms that have been passed down, or anything new that will last for future generations.

For example, the mother of the mom-to-be might bring new baby booties as well as a pair of booties she saved from her own daughter's infancy. She might bring the family christening outfit that has been used by all siblings in the family. The heirlooms could be old family photos, or simply sentiments written by the oldest member of the family to the youngest.

Gift Ideas

Baby bonnet that can be used years later as a wedding handkerchief

Silver picture frame

Patchwork quilt

Family Bible

Silver baby brush and comb set

Family tree written on archival quality paper

Engraved or monogrammed silver cup

Silver rattle or baby spoon

Keepsake Christmas ornaments

Porcelain or silver baby plate and cup

Wooden rocking horse

Engraved silver napkin rings

Heirloom jewelry or cuff links to pass down

Recipes contributed by every guest and placed in a spiral binder

Keepsake photo album

Favors Take a Polaroid picture of every guest at the shower and place it in a keepsake picture frame for them to take home.

Decorations Scour the attic or family cedar chest for old linens, doilies, and napkins—and use them! Place vintage photos of the guest of honor's family members on buffet and dining tables. Have you got a slide projector? Show slides of the guest of honor as a baby, child, and teen.

Menu Serve dishes made from favorite family recipes contributed by family and friends. The entree could be Aunt Ella's famous beef stew; the side dish might be Grandma's classic spinach and cheese casserole. Write the menu, and the name of the person who inspired each dish, on a chalkboard or piece of parchment paper for guests to read.

ABCs Shower

Guests are assigned (or choose) a letter of the alphabet, then bring a gift beginning with that letter. For example, the person assigned the letter *A* might bring an alligator puppet. A guest assigned the letter *B* could bring a bib. Help guests out with gift suggestions:

A: Alligator puppet or appliquéd baby outfit

B: Bottle warmer, baby bonnet

C: Crib bumpers, baby coat, crib sheets, clock for nursery

D: Diapers, diaper rash ointment, denim baby outfit

E: Plush elephant, electric socket safety covers

F: Toy fire truck, fringed blanket

G: Baby gate for blocking stairs and doors

H: Baby hat, high chair

I: Iridescent glow-in-the-dark planets and stars for illuminating nursery ceiling

J: Jeans outfit

K: Plush kangaroo

L: Lamp for nursery

M: Baby mittens

N: Nasal aspirator, nipples for baby bottles

O: Open-toed creeper outfit, overnight bag for mom to take to hospital

P: Perambulator (baby carriage)

Q: Quilt

R: Rubber mattress pad, receiving blanket

S: Satin-edged baby blanket, snuggly, stroller, savings bonds

T: Toys, baby thermometer

U: Underwear, umbrella stroller

V: Vinyl floor protector to place under high chair, video on baby care

W: Waffle blocks

X: Toy xylophone

Y: Anything yellow

Z: Plush zebra, zippered diaper bag

Favors ABC cookie cutters or rubber stamps with the first letter of each guest's name

Decorations Draw or paint alphabet letters on corrugated boxes or boxes of diapers, to resemble baby blocks. Visit an office supply or teacher's store and purchase oversized ABC letters or posters to hang on walls or in the party room.

Menu Serve soup made with alphabet pasta. For dessert, serve letter-shaped cookies made with alphabet cutters or sheet cakes decorated to resemble alphabet blocks.

Bib, Crib, and Booties Shower

This shower is a great idea for couples who already have had one or more children and don't need a crib, a high chair, or the major accoutrements—

but would appreciate replacement items. They sure will be able to use fresh new linens, blankets, layette items, and of course, bibs and booties. On the invitation, ask each guest to bring a pair of baby shoes or booties to be arranged in a centerpiece, and later given to the expectant mother.

Gift Ideas

Mattress pad

Coordinating sheets, blankets, bumper pads

Baby washcloths

Hooded towel

Bibs

Mobile

Receiving blankets

Nursery accessories

Infant bonnet

Booties

Changing pad and washable cover

Favors Give every guest a large bib to wear during the shower.

Decorations Fill a doll's cradle with fresh flowers or a teddy bear. Arrange an assortment of baby booties or shoes on a silver platter. Or attach ribbons to the booties or shoes and hang them from a chandelier or from tree branches placed in a vase. Depending on your color scheme, spray paint the tree branches beforehand with gold or pastel paint.

Menu Visit a florist supply shop and purchase a large booty-shaped floral holder. Use it as a serving bowl for soup, crackers, or a side dish. The menu might include soup, chicken salad, rolls, green salad, and lemon tea bread. For dessert, ask your local baker to decorate a sheet cake with baby booties; or make individual booties using cupcakes coated with frosting and fresh coconut.

To make one pair of booties, take three unfrosted cupcakes. Leave two whole to use as the heel sections of the pair. To make the protruding section for the toes, take the remaining cupcake and make a vertical slice, trimming off one-quarter of the cake. Take the remaining piece of cupcake and slice it in half horizontally. You'll have two flat semicircular pieces, each half as tall as the original cupcake. Place the trimmed flat piece against a whole cupcake. (The shape will begin to look like a booty.) Use a small bit of frosting to hold the two pieces together. Frost entire booty with pastel-tinted frosting or whipped cream, and cover with flaked coconut. Pipe decorating icing on the booties to form shoelaces, or use string licorice tied into a bow.

Bundle-of-Joy Shower

For this special party, each gift is something that can be tucked into a gift basket. Baskets could include a bundle of cloth diapers tied with a bow, baby powder, and a bottle of baby shampoo; or a bundle of crib sheets, a receiving blanket, and a rattle. Not only does the mother-to-be receive lots of baby paraphernalia, she takes home a whole collection of decorative baskets that will be useful long after the baby has arrived.

Gift Ideas

Basket of travel-size toiletries to take to the hospital

Basket of videos, popcorn, and hot cocoa mix

Basket of receiving blankets, hats, and mittens

Basket of baby shampoo, lotion, powder, washcloths, and baby brush and comb

Basket with gourmet treats for new parents

Basket of spa treatments

Nantucket Lightship Basket purse for the new mom

Bicycle basket and baby bicycle seat for Mom to take Baby on her bike

Beverage basket of coffee beans, teabags, mugs, and coffee grinder

Basket of champagne with two crystal glasses for celebrating the birth

Basket with disposable camera and prepaid developing mailer

Basket of gift certificates for take-out dinners for couple

Picnic basket filled with tablecloth, plastic plates, utensils, thermos

Favors Tiny baskets in the shape of a baby cradle

Decorations Purchase a large, trunk-size wicker basket and use it to display the shower gifts. When the party is over, give it to the new mom for use in the baby's room.

Menu Serve a meal of sandwiches, fruits, and cheeses from picnic hampers. Spread a large blanket on the floor and invite guests to picnic there. Serve beverages from hot and cold thermal containers. (Not everyone enjoys sitting on the floor, so be sure to supply some comfy chairs as well.) Use paper plates, napkins, and cups.

On-the-Road-Again Shower

If the parents travel a great deal for business or pleasure, consider a travel-theme shower. The premise here is for guests to bring travel-size gifts or baby paraphernalia perfect for setting up a nursery away from home—whether it's at grandma's house or a hotel. While it's true that many hotels and motels today have a limited number of loaner cribs on hand, parents can't always count on one being available and it's always nicer to have a portable of your own.

There are many travel-friendly products for babies on the market, including portable playpens and baby beds that collapse or can be easily dismantled for toting in a duffel bag.

Consider writing the invitation on oversized luggage tags, or print them out on a home computer to resemble a travel itinerary. For fun, write the invitation on the wings of a paper or toy airplane.

Gift Ideas

For Baby

Portable crib, mattress, and sheets

Portable high chair or baby seat that straps to a regular chair

Travel playpen

Travel car seat

Baby backpack with metal frame or baby snuggly

Travel diaper bag filled with trial-size shampoo, baby powder, diaper cream, baby brush, sealed travel-size packets of baby wipes, travel-size containers of laundry detergent

Plastic travel plates and cups with lids

Disposable diapers

Disposable bibs

Pop-top cans of baby formula

Collapsible umbrella stroller

Extra plastic bottles, nipples, bottle brush

Can opener

For parents

Travel-size coffeemaker, coffee, tea, nondairy creamer, mugs

Overnight bag or luggage on wheels

Plug-in bottle warmer

Favors Travel mug for use in a car or boat

Decorations Ask your local travel agent for travel posters, maps, or brochures. Create a large poster resembling an airport arrivals computer. The message could read: "ARRIVING: June 4, Baby Smith. GATE: Charleston Hospital. STATUS: On time."

Menu Use a food trolley to serve everyone a little bag of snack peanuts or trail mix of granola, raisins, and nuts. Follow the snack with airplane food served on little rectangular plastic plates. Give each guest a plastic knife, fork, and spoon wrapped in plastic wrap, and clear plastic cups. The menu might include steak tips with roasted peppers; rolls and butter; green salad; fruit salad; and coffee, tea, or other beverage. For dessert, serve a coconut cake cut into squares.

Remember When Shower

This party is meant to pamper the mom-to-be with gifts of comfortable clothes and accessories she can feel great in until she gets her prebaby figure back. Guests are free to bring a token gift for the baby, such as booties or a bib, but the gifts are primarily for the expectant mother—who may be feeling as if she'll never be in shape again. Even moms who can immediately fit into their old clothes will appreciate having comfortable new things to wear after the baby arrives. Look for easy-care fabrics that are machine washable and require no ironing.

Gift Ideas

Stretchy leggings

Tunic tops or oversized shirts

Nursing bra

Broomstick skirt with elastic waist

Comfort stretch slacks

Comfy slippers

Nursing nightgown

Flannel nightshirt

Elastic-waist jeans

Lingerie

Silk scarf

Jewelry

Gift certificate for manicure and pedicure

Gift certificate for hair styling

Favors Nail polish and emery board, wrapped in tulle and tied with ribbon

Decorations Place before and after pictures of the guest of honor across a fireplace mantel or long buffet table. At the left, display pictures from infancy, childhood, teens, college or work life, wedding, and early marriage. At the center, place a picture of a cute baby clipped from a magazine. At the right, display current pictures of the expectant mother in maternity clothes. At the far right, clip a magazine picture of a slim, supermodel and paste a photocopied picture of the expectant mom's face over the body. Write the message: "This is how Grace will look again after the baby! What a babe!"

Menu Serve foods women traditionally crave during pregnancy, such as ice cream and pickles. Set up a buffet with comfort foods such as lasagna, meat loaf and gravy, green salad, garlic bread, and blonde brownies.

First-Year Shower

Babies change so much during the first year! Prepare the mother-to-be with books on developmental stages and gifts geared for the first twelve months of life. These might include parenting magazines, developmentally appropriate toys, and learning tools, and gifts for the new parents to enjoy month by month.

Gift Ideas

First month: Diapers, diaper rash ointment, baby bath, bedding

Second: Books on baby care, gift certificates for take-out dinners for parents

Third: Gym or fitness club membership for parents

Fourth: Baby rice, plate, spoon

Fifth: Gift certificate for baby portrait

Sixth: Weekend getaway for parents

Seventh: Plastic sipping cup for baby

Eighth: Safety items such as electric socket covers and door gates to baby-proof the house

Ninth: Teething ring, rattle, salve, or ointment to soothe baby's sore gums

Tenth: Baby shoes for those first few steps

Eleventh: Gift certificate for family portrait

Twelfth: First-birthday presents, birthday celebration packet with hats and streamers

Favors Pocket calendar

We want to host a shower for an expectant friend, but her mother is superstitious about having a shower before the baby is born. She is worried something might go wrong, and that her daughter would be heartbroken with all those baby things around. What should we do?

In this situation, avoid planning a surprise shower. Instead, directly ask the mother-to-be what scenario *she'd* prefer: a shower before or after the baby is born. She may not share her mother's misgivings. It's important to realize that in some cultures, it's considered bad luck to "tempt fate" and start celebrating the birth of a child before it arrives. Her mother might have known someone who experienced the trauma of miscarriage or complications and remember their heartbreak. Be sensitive. Don't push. It's just as much fun to have a shower *after* the baby arrives—and the bonus is that baby can attend, too!

Decorations Clip magazine photographs of babies from birth through age one and display on the walls. Take a large sheet of poster board or a roll of white craft paper and make a time line of the baby's first year. Have guests fill in each month with the landmarks their own children reached, such as "Timmy first rolled over when he was four months. Allison started to walk at eleven months." If some of the guests don't have children, have them fill in facts they know about their own childhoods, "Mom says I didn't get my first tooth until I was fourteen months old."

Menu Serve baby teething biscuits as appetizers. Arrange a buffet of cold cuts, macaroni salad, potato salad, several varieties of bread, and condiments including mustard, mayonnaise, and pickles.

Show-Me-How Shower

For the first-time mother who doesn't have a clue how to care for a baby, this shower offers a lot of fun and a fountain of practical wisdom Ask each guest to arrive with a gift and his or her best tip for doing something better. It's amazing what parents can teach each other!

For example, one guest might demonstrate how to change a diaper; another could show how to check the temperature of a bottle; another might teach everyone how to bathe a baby. (Ask another new mom attending the party if you can borrow her baby for the demonstration.) While these baby-care skills are things that usually are taught in the hospital, new mothers are often so tired after the birth that they don't remember the information and techniques once they get home. And seasoned parents know all the best tricks for changing sheets with one hand or making up the bed with alternating layers of cloth sheet and rubber sheet so that cleaning up leaks will be a breeze. (You pull off the wet layers and the crib is already made.)

Be Prepared by Learning First Aid and CPR

Consider inviting a certified professional to teach important first-aid skills such as infant cardiopulmonary resuscitation (CPR) or first aid for choking. When my first child was less than five weeks old, she narrowly survived an episode in which she suddenly stopped breathing while sleeping. She turned blue. Luckily, my husband stayed up late that night and checked her crib before it was too late. He was able to revive her, and we immediately sought neonatal treatment at the local hospital. Following that near-death experience, we both learned infant first aid and CPR; we now firmly believe those skills are the greatest gift you can give to any new parents.

Assign someone to photograph or videotape guests as they share their words of wisdom, or ask them to take notes in a keepsake scrapbook. Guests who are not parents can share a fond memory of how their parents raised them, such as "My mom always read me a story before she tucked us into bed. I loved it."

Calculate the number of years the guests have collectively been parents—or children themselves—and impress them with the result: "Do you all realize that together we have been parents for more than 163 years!"

Present the guest of honor with a list of the names, phone numbers, and E-mail addresses of all the guests, so that she has a support network to call for advice after the baby is born.

Gift Ideas

Baby-care books

Family medical handbook

Parenting advice books

Household first-aid kit

Phone card

Cell phone

Wipe-clean baby-sitter's message and information board

Subscription to a parenting magazine

Favors Baby bottle filled with chocolate kisses

Decorations Make a cabbage patch by arranging fresh green and purple cabbages of varying sizes. Arrange baby dolls between the cabbages. On a small sign or cardboard card, write "Where Babies Come From."

Menu Serve an informal meal of hot dogs, hamburgers, french fries, crudité, and potato chips. Use a plastic baby bottle as a ketchup dispenser, and cut a large hole in the top of the nipple for easy serving. Place mustard and relish in cleaned-out baby food jars. Wrap pink and blue ribbons around the jars.

Are there any rules for hosting a baby shower?

Rules—no; guidelines—yes. Generally, showers are held in the month or two before the baby is due or at least a month after the baby is born. (How many baby showers have you been to where the expectant mom is just barely a few weeks pregnant or just delivered the baby a few weeks ago and is still bleary-eyed and sleep-deprived?) Keep in mind that if the mother-to-be is bedridden during pregnancy or feels extremely unwell or uncomfortable, she may not feel up to a big party. If the shower date is scheduled too close to the baby's due date, the mom may be a no-show. Babies have been known to arrive early.

6

Specialty Showers

Brides and expectant mothers aren't the only people who deserve showers! Host a shower for any loved one who needs a party, a show of support, or just a new set of dishes to replace the chipped ones.

Instead of a dreary retirement party, make it a Retiree Shower. Brighten the day of a sick friend with a Chapeau Shower. Instead of a ho-hum graduation party, fete your favorite freshman-to-be with a Groom-Your-Room Shower that will make him the hit of the dormitory. Celebrate a long-married friend's anniversary with an Anniversary Shower.

Retiree Shower

Retiree Showers, like baby and bridal showers, are for people celebrating a major life transition. Whether a friend or loved one is marrying, becoming a parent, or embarking on the journey through the golden years, he or she deserves a special celebration and a shower of presents to help mark that passage.

Honor the retiree with a testimonial dinner or This-Is-Your-Life Shower featuring childhood photographs, surprise guests, and reflections on his or her achievements or family milestones. Write the invitations on manila business stationery in the style of a business memo. Or write them on a toy boat with the message "Join Us for Maggie's Send-off." A nice group gift might be a weekend for two in the country or a gift certificate for a short cruise.

Gift Ideas

Travel guides and foreign phrase books for those trips the retiree finally has time to take

Hobby-related items, such as golf clubs, fishing lures, gardening tools

Sweat suit for lounging around

Items to stock a workbench, such as tools, lumber, paint, brushes

Items to stock a new home or second home, such as kitchenware, bedding, sheets, towels

Items to stock a potting shed, such as plant materials, pots, gardening gloves, potting soil

Theater or symphony subscription

Rocking chair or reclining lounge chair

Gift certificate to a favorite restaurant

Hammock or porch furniture

Humorous book about retirement

Subscription to a travel or leisure magazine

List of all local businesses offering senior discounts

Photo album with pictures of coworkers

Scrapbook with personal messages from well wishers

Crossword puzzle books

Needlework or hooked rug kit

Luggage and travel-size toiletries

Address book already filled in with names, E-mail addresses, and
phone number of friends and coworkers

Gag Gifts Vitamins, support hose, denture cleanser

Favors Toy gold watches from a novelty or party store

Decorations Use a desktop publishing program to create a mock newspaper page with headline proclaiming "Jim Finally Retires—After 100
Years!" Use a scanner to create a photo of the guest of honor, and have
guests contribute silly or serious articles about him or her. Decorate the
table or walls with copies of the newspaper or distribute them as
favors.

Visit the local travel agency and ask for travel guides and posters
that can be displayed on the walls. Ask coworkers for old pictures of
the honoree from the earliest days of his or her career. Take the photo
to a print or graphics shop and have it scanned and printed on paper,
or blown up and mounted on poster board. Encourage guests to write
silly messages with sentiments such as "This is Jim when he still had
hair!" or "Look at that groovy wide tie and mod boots!"

Centerpieces might be related to the honoree's hobbies or interests. Try a child's plastic bucket or glass bowl filled with swimming
goldfish and a hand-lettered "Gone Fishing" sign for an avid fisher-
man; a toy horse and racing forms for a racing fan; a metal watering

can filled with fresh flowers for a gardener; or a tweed cap, pipe, and magnifying glass for a mystery novel aficionado.

Menu Type or print a menu with the phrase "Early Bird Special!" at the top and give a joke list of dishes to be served: oatmeal, Alka-Seltzer, mashed potatoes, pork and beans, warm milk, bran, Jell-O. Then surprise everyone with a fabulous meal of grilled steaks, spinach salad with bacon dressing, baked potatoes, corn on the cob, and chocolate cake.

Fire Shower

Anyone who has ever lived through a house fire, be it a stove-top burn incident or a major conflagration, knows it is a traumatic experience. As if losing your home or belongings isn't painful enough, there is major cleanup involved in repairing the fire, smoke, and water damage. Help with the heavy work will surely be appreciated. You can also pitch in to help your friend or loved one restock, repair, or rebuild the damaged home. A Fire Shower is a loving way to turn disaster into a show of strength and support.

Begin by thinking about what was lost. Does the individual or family need immediate shelter? Clothing? Blankets? Food? Household items? Depending on the severity of the situation, it may not be appropriate or appreciated to have a party immediately after the loss.

Take some time to think about when the help is most needed. The family might need some time to recover; they almost surely will not be able to handle a surprise party. This is especially true if anyone was injured in the fire. Use your judgment about whether to throw a low-key party or a blowout bash in which people will make the best of the bad situation by celebrating their community spirit.

Consider inviting the firefighters who helped douse the blaze. They'll appreciate being recognized for their heroism, and the fire victims will get a chance to thank them.

Gift Ideas

Household basics such as sheets, towels, linens, blankets, and bedding

Kitchen items such as canned goods, small appliances, glassware, plates, cups, flatware, cooking utensils, pots and pans, storage containers, and bowls

Chairs, tables, lamps, carpets, and extension cords

Film, a camera, and a photo album for rebuilding memories

Smoke detectors

Fireproof safe

Gift certificates for helping with the major cleanup ("This certificate entitles the bearer to a full day of help cleaning rugs and walls, or whatever you wish.")

Favors Plastic red fire helmets, water bottles

Decorations Use a child's toy fire truck as a centerpiece; or fill a metal water bucket or watering can with moss and fresh flowers and write "In Case of Fire" across the side.

Menu Cold beer, three-alarm chili, barbecued ribs with hot sauce, coleslaw, french fries, flaming cherries jubilee, and toasted marshmallows

Chapeau Shower

When someone you care about is recovering from surgery or a major illness, rally the troops for a get-well shower. It could be a shower in the hospital room (get permission from the medical staff first) complete with

Is it all right to give a shower for a friend who has lost everything in a fire? It's sort of untraditional and people might object to throwing a shower for a person who has been married for thirty years.

Do it anyway! Starting over following any traumatic event—be it a fire, a divorce, or relocation—is never easy, at any age. What better way to show your loving support for your friend than to help with the expense and hassle of outfitting a home with the basics. Mail those invitations!

"hospital food" such as Jell-O, pudding, and ginger ale for everyone, or a shower at home while they're recuperating and really welcome visitors.

The Chapeau Shower was invented by a group of women who got together to buy hats for a friend who had breast cancer. The woman had lost her hair while undergoing chemotherapy and was wearing scarves and baseball caps until her locks grew back. Her friends decided to throw a special shower to help cheer her up and urged every guest to bring her a hat.

The fun part is taking pictures of everyone trying on all the hats. Bring along a Polaroid camera and props such as feather boas, gloves, sunglasses, and movie star–style cigarette holders, then have everyone pose for silly keepsake shots. The guest of honor will go home with a scrapbook and a wardrobe of gorgeous hats.

Gifts Ideas

Scarves

Wigs, hairpieces, or hair extensions in neon colors or the guest of honor's natural color

Beret and "movie star" sunglasses

Fedora

Hat rack

Soft turban wrap hat

Baseball cap with logo of guest of honor's favorite team

Wide-brimmed straw hat

Pillbox hat

Old-fashioned hatbox

Cloche

Top hat

Gag Gifts Baby bonnet, plastic red fire helmet, cowboy hat, Indiana Jones–style hat, vintage hat with fake cherries or birds

Favors Hat pins, hatboxes, berets, sunglasses, or gloves

Decorations Hang movie posters of cinema idols wearing glamorous hats or pictures of the Queen of England in one of her many hats.

Menu Find a talented baker to make a cake in the shape of a hat. Or serve dessert in little plastic baseball caps or top hats, available at craft outlets and party stores. For a centerpiece, place a pretty straw hat with satin bow in the center of the buffet table. Use an inverted top hat (a real one or a plastic one from a craft outlet or party store) as a holder for forks, knives, and spoons. If the hostess favors French berets, serve a French-style cassoulet or casserole, French onion soup, French bread, green salad, and little Madeleine sponge cakes or cream puffs.

Groom-Your-Room Shower

Instead of a traditional graduation party for the high school grad going off to college, host a Groom-Your-Room Shower. Sure, every student *needs* a dictionary and thesaurus, but most of them will *appreciate* dorm room necessities much more. By the time they've unpacked on the first day of college, they'll feel immediately at home, and their comfy room will be a magnet for new friends.

Using a home computer, create invitations to look like report cards or graduation diplomas. Advise guests to bring anything that will help to make a dorm room a home away from home.

Gift Ideas

Extra-long twin sheets, since most dorm beds are longer than the standard twin

Comforter, towels, throw rug

Prepaid phone card

Lamp

Pillow

Mirror

Curtains

Bulletin board

Small television

Miniature refrigerator

Small microwave

Iron

Popcorn maker

Footlocker

Rocking chair

Shelves

Storage containers

Plastic bucket for toting toilet articles to the shower

Care package with can opener, pop-top soups, tuna, hot cocoa mix, Ziploc bags, candy, popcorn, tea, coffee, nondairy creamer, mugs, bowls, loose change for the laundry room, laundry detergent, gift certificates to restaurants and shops located in the college town or area

Gag Gifts Children's ABCs book or oversize eraser

Favors Crayons, pencil case, miniature chalkboard, assignment book

Menu Cold drinks served in frosted mugs, dining hall food such as meat loaf, mashed potatoes with gravy, pizza served directly from the box, and dorm-style grilled cheese sandwiches. College students make them by placing a slice of yellow American cheese between two slices of buttered bread, wrapping the sandwich in aluminum foil, and melting the cheese by ironing the packet with an iron on low setting. But, you can make them the old-fashioned way with a skillet.

Relocation Shower

When a friend announces she's been transferred to another part of the country for work, or just wants to experience life in a new city, break out the invitations and throw a party. After all, you're not losing a friend, you're gaining a place to visit.

Find out everything you can about the guest of honor's new hometown by searching the Internet or contacting the local convention center or tourism board. Collect brochures, maps, coupons from the local retailers, and information on special attractions there and insert them in a loose-leaf binder as a gift to the guest of honor. Cut up colorful old maps to use as place mats or tablecloths.

Write the invitations on the back of luggage tags; or attach the invitation to tiny matchbox cars with the message "Ann's Moving; Come Along for the Ride!" Or write the invitation as an itinerary slipped into an airline ticket holder from a travel agency or one made from construction paper.

Gift Ideas

Local road atlas and city maps from their new town

List of sightseeing and attractions in the new town (call the local chamber of commerce)

Gift certificates for restaurants and shops in the new town

Luggage

Travel alarm clock

Address book filled with names, phone numbers, and E-mail addresses of friends and family

Stamps and custom stationery printed with the guest of honor's new address

Artist's rendering of the home the guest of honor will be leaving

Plane tickets for a reunion trip in six months

Favors Tote bags filled with travel-size soaps and toiletries

Decorations Fill the room with large packing boxes and luggage. Use an old trunk as a serving table for hors d'oeuvres or drinks.

Menu Consider hosting a progressive dinner party in which guests visit one home for cocktails, another for dinner, and another for dessert. If the season permits, plan an outdoor picnic at a beach, park, or pool.

Got-the-Sack Shower

In this day of high-tech companies and mega-mergers, many people lose their jobs at least once in their career, whether from downsizing, being fired, or getting laid off when a company goes under or gets bought out. Don't pout—party! A job crisis can bring unexpected opportunity. Help the guest of honor keep his or her chin up by hosting a Got-the-Sack Shower.

Invite coworkers, friends, and loved ones who will be supportive. Write the invitations on small brown paper lunch sacks or index cards. Tuck a Rolodex card into each invitation and ask friends to bring the names and phone numbers of at least five people they think might help the guest of honor find another job.

Three Gifts for a New Home

According to ancient tradition, give friends these three gifts to ensure happiness in a new home: a loaf of bread, so that the family will never go hungry; a broom, to sweep the new home clean of all sorrow; and a box of salt, to add spice to their lives.

Consider inviting a psychic or fortune-teller to entertain guests with tarot card readings or fortune-telling sessions. Losing a job can make anyone feel inadequate, so have guests toast the honoree by citing his or her personal achievements and good qualities. "Jim, here's to your bright future! You are a great salesman, a valued neighbor, and you make the very best martinis I've ever tasted."

Gift Ideas

Briefcase

Wristwatch ("to remind the honoree that there are better times ahead")

Book on writing a resume

Gift certificate for a session with career counselor

Gift certificate for business attire

Tickets to a show or gift certificates to the movies

Coupon for a free round of golf or a manicure and pedicure

Book of inspirational sayings

Humorous book

Gift certificate for a weekend getaway

Phone cards for free long-distance calls

Favors Scratch-off "instant win" lottery cards

Decorations Write a glowing resume of the guest of honor's sterling qualities and blow it up to poster size. Include his or her name and special skills; these can be either serious or silly: "Best friend a guy ever had," "The best baker on the block," "Gives the most relaxing back rubs of anyone we know."

Menu Find out what the guest of honor's favorite meal is and make it from scratch.

Empty Nest Shower

The kids are finally grown up and gone. What's a parent to do? Have a party! Help your friends launch this next phase of their lives with an Empty Nest Shower. Isn't it about time they turned the extra bedroom into a sewing room or den? Or finally took the time to cultivate a new hobby or a new career? Help them do it, or provide the gifts that will shower them with inspiration.

Help a friend adjust to the new solo lifestyle by inviting him or her out a few nights a week—maybe for a potluck dinner or to see a movie. Or form a Monday Night Dinner Group with a bunch of other people who would enjoy good food and good company. Take turns having the dinner at a different person's house each week.

Many newcomer clubs welcome empty nesters even if they aren't new to the community. Find out when the local newcomers club meets and make a list of its upcoming day trips, athletic groups, social activities, and subsidiary clubs.

Write the invitations on wooden birdhouse ornaments, available from craft or holiday stores. Or tuck feathers or plastic eggs into the envelope, along with a message: "Helen's kids have flown the coop. Help us feather her nest with a surprise shower."

Gift Ideas

Class schedule from a local community college or continuing education program

Travel books

Craft supplies or hobby materials

Delivery of a week's worth of cooked meals

A live pet (Be careful here. First determine whether or not the person is allergic to animals and find out whether they would enjoy one.)

Subscription to a magazine

Annual membership to a museum or theater series

Cooking lessons

Interior decorating classes

Gardening tools and implements

Favors Miniature birdhouses

Decorations Purchase a faux bird's nest at a craft store and fill it with candy eggs and tiny decorative birds. Scour tag sales and antique shops

---

A friend just went through a terrible divorce. She's devastated. She's lost her house and is starting over. Is it in poor taste to celebrate with a shower when, after all, her marriage is over?

Think of it this way, you aren't celebrating the end of her marriage but rather helping her to establish a new life. This is the time when she can use a shower of love and support—not to mention a new blender, toaster, and other household stuff, too.

for old bird cages. Fill them with moss or green plants and hang from the ceiling or suspend from the front porch.

Menu Egg drop soup, egg salad, baked chicken, corn bread, steamed carrots, chocolate cream pie

Single-and-Loving-It Shower

Engaged couples aren't the only ones who could use a shower of gifts. Ask anyone who is single and desperately needs a toaster or a new can opener. Those who remain single, by choice or chance, will relish a shower instead of a ho-hum birthday party. Give all the traditional gifts associated with bridal showers, such as toasters, blenders, and electric blankets. This shower could be given for one guest, or a circle of single friends might gather to exchange gifts with each other.

Divorce Shower

Here's your chance to lift the spirits of a friend who has survived a tumultuous divorce. Divorce is never pretty, but a party often can help to take some of the sting out of it. It also will remind the showeree of all the love and support in his or her life. Gifts might be silly gag items such as humorous books or practical household basics and furnishings to start a new life. Write the invitations on blue legal paper. Have guests make a list of all the advantages of being single: "You can eat crackers in bed," "No one tells you to turn off the light and go to sleep," "You can turn up the volume on the stereo as loud as you want," "You can drink milk directly from the container and no one bugs you." At the shower, play pop tunes with inspiring messages such as "I am Free!" (The Who) or "I Will Survive" (Gloria Gaynor).

Anniversary Shower

Anyone who's been married a long time can tell you: blenders break down, china gets chipped, and blankets wear out. The next time you're planning an anniversary party, make it a shower. Ask guests to bring all the traditional gifts they would bring for a bridal shower—the can openers, tablecloths, toasters, and teapots. It's a great way to restock the kitchen or bed and bath—and to lift the spirits. The guest of honor will feel like a young bride again, even if she's been married for thirty years.

7

Shower Games

SHOWERS AND CHILDREN'S parties have one thing in common: playing games is part of the fun. It's traditional for showers to include games and activities—ranging from silly to bawdy. Maybe it's because showers typically include guests who have never met before and may never meet again. Shower games are a wonderful way to break the ice and encourage interaction and conversation among guests. Where else but a shower would perfect strangers be expected to drink from a baby bottle or watch each other make wedding veils from rolls of toilet paper?

When planning activities, keep in mind the tone of your crowd. Will they find games hilarious or annoying? Will they jump in and participate or will they need to be coerced? Remember, it isn't written in stone that all showers include shower games—and some crowds downright resent them.

It's important to think twice about games that might embarrass guests or make them feel foolish. If you think the bride's future mother-in-law or prissy Aunt Bess will be horrified by games or gag gifts with sexual over-tones, skip them in favor of tamer games. At a shower everyone should have fun and feel comfortable.

Games Suitable for Any Type of Shower

If the shower game is a competition of sorts and warrants a prize, make it useful or thoughtful, rather than something that will be tossed into the trash. Wrap each prize as a token present and the winners will feel special. Prizes might include a small cookbook, a cosmetics bag, a movie theater gift certificate, pretty notepaper, a minisewing kit for purse or desk, temporary "press-on" tattoos, scented powder, or a disposable camera.

Time Line

Ask the guests to stand and arrange themselves in a single line—from the person who has known the guest of honor the longest time to the person who has known him or her for the shortest time. This is a wonderful way to loosen people up—they have to get to know each other to figure out where each one goes in the line. When the line is completed, each guest shares a memory about what the friendship or relationship means. Set a limit on how much time each guest has to speak—people really get into this and love to chatter on and on. (Don't forget to take a picture of the whole lineup!)

Who Am I?

This is a classic shower game. Purchase index cards and write the name of a famous person on each one. Attach a card to each guest's back with tape or a pin. Tell the guests to wander around and look at the names on the backs of the other players. Each player is allowed to ask the group five yes-or-no questions per round about their identity. Questions might include "Am I a movie star?" "Am I living?" "Am I a politician?" It takes several rounds until players get enough information to make a guess. The first person to guess the name on his or her back wins the game.

Take It Off

Have on hand as many large paper grocery bags or big paper (not plastic!) shopping bags as there are guests. Punch large holes in each bag for eyes and nose and mouth. Give all guests a bag and tell them to place it over their head. Then ask each guest to take off one thing they don't need. It's hilarious to watch guests remove their shoes, jewelry, hose, or even under-slips before they realize they don't need the bag on their head! Whoever takes the bag off first is declared the winner.

Shower Bingo

Using a home computer, or simply drawing it yourself, make up bingo "cards" with the letters *B-I-N-G-O* across the top and horizontal and vertical lines creating twenty-five boxes (five rows across and five rows down). Mark at least one box a free space and leave the others blank. At the beginning of the shower, tell guests to fill in all the boxes with their predictions for gifts the guest of honor will receive, such as "baby booties" or "crib bumpers" for a baby shower or "crystal vase" and "bath towels" for a bridal shower. As the guest of honor opens gifts, the guest crosses out any gifts she or he accurately predicted. The first guest to get a BINGO (a full line across, up and down, or diagonally) wins.

My Favorite Memory

Ask each guest to recall his or her fondest memory of the guest of honor. They might talk about when they first met, or an incident they'll never forget. ("Bob, when we were younger, you always stuck up for me with the school bully. I'm sure you'll make a great husband and father.") Be sure to have someone videotape or write down the sentiments, and keep a box of tissues on hand. This shower game can get emotional.

Did You Know?

This is a great icebreaker. Once all the guests have arrived, ask them to introduce themselves and tell one thing about them that even their families might not know. Assure them it doesn't have to be anything embarrassing or revealing. For example, "Hi, my name is Alice, I am seventy-two years old and I have always wanted to go skydiving!" or "My name is Betsy, and I love to make quilts."

Scrapbook Sayings

As guests arrive, take their pictures with a Polaroid or digital camera. Give each person a page from a scrapbook and ask for a written sentiment to the guest of honor. As the gifts are opened, each guest places his or her page into the keepsake scrapbook. Be sure to purchase a scrapbook with archival quality paper—that is, paper that is acid-free and lignin-free and less susceptible to deterioration over time.

Pack Rats

Make a list of odd items and see if any of the guests are carrying them in their pockets, purses, or briefcases. Items might include:

A piece of fruit

A stick of gum

A screwdriver

A hard-boiled egg

A canceled stamp

An emery board

Duct tape

Foreign coins or currency

An unsharpened pencil

An eyeglass repair kit

A floppy disk

Breath mints

More than one key chain

A picture of an old girlfriend or boyfriend

A picture of a pet

A button

A name tag

Anything laminated

A form of birth control

A paperback book

Nails or screws

A roll of tape

A green pen or marker

A plastic spoon or fork

The person with the most number of items on hand wins the game.

Shower Jeopardy

Before the party, collaborate with relatives or friends of the guest of honor to make a list of insider information about the guest of honor for guests to answer in two teams. As in the "Jeopardy" television show, the answers must be in question form. For example, in the pets category, guests might be challenged to devise the right question for "He had floppy ears and a wet nose." The answer: "Who was Jane's beagle Sparky?" The team that knows the most about the guest of honor wins. Categories might include:

Family and Friends

Childhood Stories

The College (or Work) Years

Old Boyfriends

Pet Peeves

Fashion Goofs

Favorites (color, food, car, travel destination, book, or movie)

Pets

Nicknames

Write a Caption

Before the party, collect at least a dozen photographs of the guest of honor—from childhood to the present—and make a photocopy of each. Tape each photo to the wall and invite guests to write funny or silly captions underneath each. For a photo of the guest of honor dressed up in a school uniform for the first day of kindergarten, the caption might be: "Here is John in his very first business suit. Check out those polished shoes and the crisp white shirt."

Games for Bridal Showers

Games seem to be as much a part of bridal showers as cake and presents. Let guests arrive, grab a drink, and mingle first before launching into a game. Unlike most other parties, showers tend to bring together groups of people who might not know each other, such as the bride's family, coworkers, future in-laws, or school chums. You might schedule a few party games before the meal is served or the gifts are opened to give people a chance to loosen up and meet each other in a relaxed setting.

Words of Wisdom

Professional party planner Roberta Sekas of Custom Party Creations in Orange, Connecticut, shares this popular bridal shower game:

"All the guests stand in a circle with an unlit candle. The bride's candle is then lit first. As she stands in front of each guest, they give her words of wisdom. These words could pertain to her personally, or they might constitute a recipe for a healthy marriage. This can be a very sentimental moment. Once the guest is finished dispensing words of wisdom, the bride lights his or her candle and proceeds to the next guest. Someone should be appointed to write down what each guest says. When all the guests have given their words of wisdom, the bride is presented with a guest book with the words written down from each person. The guest book also serves as memorabilia; she may include friends who were unable to attend the shower. Finally, the shower ends with a prayer for the bride's happiness."

(Note: This game can also be modified for a baby shower. The mother-to-be's candle is the first one lit, and guests give her words of wisdom about raising a child and being a good parent.)

Great Romances

Have guests play a game of romance trivia. Whoever gets the most correct answers wins a bottle of champagne or box of chocolate kisses.

1. Name two famous actors or comedians who are also a married couple. (Answers might include: *Jerry Stiller and Anne Meara; Anne Bancroft and Mel Brooks; Joseph Bologna and Renee Taylor; Joanne Woodward and Paul Newman; Brad Pitt and Jennifer Aniston.*)

2. Who was Dick Tracy's girlfriend?
Tess Trueheart

3. Who was Fred Flintstone's Stone Age wife?
Wilma

4. What is the name of Regis Philbin's actress/talk show host wife?
Joy Philbin

5. Which famous actress married to Clark Gable was killed in a plane crash?
Carole Lombard

6. Which famous actress "stole" actress Debbie Fisher's husband?
Elizabeth Taylor

7. What kind of gemstone did the late Princess Diana have for an engagement ring?
blue sapphire

8. Who was the love of Miss Piggy's life?
Kermit the Frog

9. Name the biblical vixen responsible for cutting off Samson's hair.
Delilah

10. Name both of Donald Trump's wives.
Ivana Trump and Marla Maples-Trump

11. Which actors played lovers in the films *Romancing the Stone* and *Jewel of the Nile*?
Michael Douglas and Kathleen Turner

12. In the *Addams Family* movie and TV series, what was the name of Gomez Addams's wife?
Morticia Addams

13. What are the names of the husband and wife who comprised the detective team in the Thin Man novels by Dashiell Hammett?
Nick and Nora Charles

14. What was the name of their pet dog?
Asta

15. What was the name of the woman whose love affair "launched a thousand ships"?
Helen of Troy

16. In the film *An Affair to Remember* at what famous New York landmark were the characters played by Cary Grant and Deborah Kerr supposed to rendezvous?
Empire State Building

What's My Word?

Party planner Roberta Sekas offers another fun shower game, What's My Word? Here's how it works. Before the shower, make a list of wedding-related words (*gown*, *honeymoon*, *love*, *groom's name*, and so forth). Write these words on name tags, and give one to each arriving guest. The guest is not allowed to say the word that's on his or her name tag. If someone hears him or her say the word, that person takes the name tag away from the person who said the prohibited word. At the end of the shower, the person with the most name tags win a prize. "This game never ceases to amaze me," Sekas says. "Inevitably the quietest, shyest guest will race across the room in pursuit of someone else's name tag."

Pop the Balloon!

Provide each guest with a balloon to blow up, tie, and break. Inside each balloon is a strip of paper that has a simple saying. Only one balloon will have the wedding date written on it. The person who receives the wedding date wins a prize. You need to purchase twelve-inch white balloons and insert strips of paper inside. Sayings that you can write on the paper strips may include "Too bad," "Better luck next time," "Sorry, no cigar," "Nothing for you," and so forth. It's great to watch participants try to pop the balloons by sitting, standing, and stomping—without using sharp objects. Latex balloons work the best, as they are a little harder to break.

Operator

The shower guests sit in a circle. The person to the left of the bride begins by saying his or her first name and an imaginary gift that begins with the first letter of the name. For example, "My name is Terry and I am going to Barbara's bridal shower and I brought towels." The next person in the circle has to name a gift beginning with the first word of her own name, and *also* repeat what the person before her said. ("My name is Patty and I am going to Barbara's bridal shower and I brought place mats and Terry brought towels.") Continue around the circle with each person saying his or her name and gift and also reciting the names and gifts of the people who already took a turn. Whoever forgets an item in the ever-growing list leaves the circle. The last person remaining is the winner.

Here Comes the Bride

Fill a big cardboard box with ribbons, glue, lace, sequins, and other decorations. Give each guest a roll of toilet paper and two bobby pins and challenge them to make a bridal veil. They use only the toilet paper and items from the cardboard box. Ask the bride to choose which veil is the prettiest, silliest, or most outrageous or original. The winner gets a prize.

As the Years Go By

Challenge guests to name the traditional and contemporary gifts that are associated with each wedding anniversary. Give them about ten minutes to fill in the list. The person with the most correct answers wins a prize. The anniversary gift list comes from *Bride's Wedding Planner* by the editors of *Brides* magazine.

Traditional	*Contemporary*
1st Paper	1st Clock
2nd Cotton	2nd China
3rd Leather	3rd Crystal or glass
4th Linen	4th Electrical appliance
5th Wood	5th Silverware
6th Iron	6th Wood
7th Wool	7th Desk set
8th Bronze	8th Linens or lace
9th Pottery	9th Leather
10th Tin or aluminum	10th Diamond jewelry
11th Steel	11th Fashion accessories
12th Silk	12th Pearls
13th Lace	13th Textiles or fur
14th Ivory	14th Gold jewelry
15th Crystal	15th Watches
20th China	20th Platinum
25th Silver	25th Sterling silver
30th Pearls	30th Diamonds
35th Coral or jade	35th Jade

40th Rubies	40th Rubies
45th Sapphires	45th Sapphires
50th Emeralds	55th Emeralds
60th Diamonds	60th Diamonds

Wedding Night Phrases

As the bride opens gifts, one guest records her reactions and exclamations, such as "Oh, I will enjoy this again and again!" or "This is such a big present!" Later, the list is read back with the preface, "These are things that Gigi and Mark might say to each other on their wedding night." (Remember, this double entendre game can get a little bawdy and the sexual innuendoes might embarrass some guests. If you think anyone might be offended, choose another game instead.)

Pass the Bouquet

In this bridal version of musical chairs, "Here Comes the Bride" is played while guests stand in a circle and pass a floral bouquet from person to person. The person holding the bouquet when the music stops must leave the circle. Keep repeating the passing-and-stopping routine until the last person left in the circle is declared the winner. The winner gets a prize of a fresh bouquet or floral arrangement.

Here Comes Which Bride?

Before the shower, ask all the guests to make a copy of their wedding portrait, or their parents' or grandparents' wedding photograph. As guests arrive, have them pin their photo to their clothing. Conversations will start quickly and easily as everyone asks about the photos and comments on the changing gown styles. Challenge guests to guess the year in which each pictured couple was married. The guest with the most correct answers wins a picture frame.

The Nearly Newlyweds Game

This game is perfect for a coed Jack-and-Jill Shower attended by the bride- and groom-to-be and their friends. Ask the groom some funny questions ahead of time. Then challenge the bride to say what she thinks he answered. Sample questions might include:

Jim, how would Brenda describe you as a kisser? Are you Don Juan, Don Johnson, or Donny Osmond?

How many blind dates has Brenda gone on in her lifetime?

How many long-sleeve sweaters does Brenda own?

What are the names of the Great Lakes?

What was Brenda wearing on the day you met?

What was your first meal together?

Where did you go on your third date?

Name five things she always has in her refrigerator.

What is the most recent book she read?

How would Brenda answer this question? I love John because he is _____ and _____ and _____.

Games for Baby Showers

Most people enjoy a little silliness during a baby shower. Have a few prizes on hand to make it more fun. Choices might include a phone card, a bottle of bath salts, a manicure set, or any other small, useful item.

Mum's the Word

Liz Pisaretz contributes this game, which all guests can easily play. As each guest arrives, she is handed a diaper pin. The object is to see how long each person can go without saying the word *baby*. If *baby* (or *babies*) is said, the person who said it gives up her diaper pin. It's lots of fun to see how each person avoids saying the *B* word and makes up new phrases to replace it in a sentence. At the end of the shower, the person with the most diaper pins is awarded a prize, which can be one of the table arrangements or any number of small gift items.

Diaper Derby

For this game, you'll need a doll at least twelve to fourteen inches tall, one cloth diaper, two diaper pins, a pair of woolen mittens, and a stopwatch or wristwatch that measures seconds. Guests take turns diapering the baby while wearing the mittens! Prizes are awarded for fastest or neatest diapering. A variation on this is to blindfold the guests before they begin diapering!

What's My Jar?

Before the shower, purchase a dozen jars of pureed baby food. Cover or remove the labels and number the jars, but don't open them. Guests take turns guessing the type of food inside each jar. The contestant with the most correct answers wins. As a variation, take the lids off and let each person taste the food before guessing! This is hilarious, especially watching their faces as they sample pureed liver or mushy veggies!

Celebrity Parent

Make a list of celebrities and the names of their offspring. The first guest to match up all the famous moms or dads with their son or daughter wins. You might include these famous people and their children:

Madonna	Lourdes and Rocco
Kate Winslet	Mia
Blythe Danner	Gwyneth (Paltrow)
Janet Leigh	Jamie Lee (Curtis)
Don Ho	Hoku
Kathie Lee Gifford	Cody and Cassidy
Naomi Judd	Wynona and Ashley
Bruce Dern	Laura
Kirk Douglas	Michael
Frank Zappa	Moon Unit and Dweezil

Cher	Chastity and Elijah Blue
Debbie Reynolds	Carrie Fisher
Cybil Shepherd	Clementine
Jerry Seinfeld	Sascha

Baby Bottle Race

Purchase one plastic baby bottle per guest. Fill the bottles with juice or iced tea. Challenge guests to a race to see who can empty his or her bottle the fastest. This makes for a humorous photograph of all those grown-ups sucking on baby bottles!

Happy Birthday

As guests arrive, ask them the day and month of their birthday. Whoever's birthday is closest to the baby's due date, or actual birth date if the baby has already been born, wins.

Memory Game

Before guests arrive, place a variety of small baby-related items on a tray where guests can easily see them. Items might include a pacifier, diaper, baby brush and comb, diaper pins, booties, socks, bonnet, bottle cleaning brush, nail clippers, bath toy, sponge, or stuffed toy. During the party, tell guests you are going to play a memory game and cover up the tray. Then make up a ruse for the expectant mom to leave the room for a moment. You might ask her to get more cups or napkins, and so on. Guests will think they have to name the items on the tray—but the game is to ask them to describe what the guest of honor was wearing, from her shoes and hose to her jacket, slacks, blouse, hair barrettes, purse, or whatever. The person with the most correct answers wins.

Name That Baby

Before the shower, ask guests to bring a baby picture of themselves to the party. Place all the pictures on the buffet table or a fireplace mantel and challenge people to match the guests with their childhood photos. The guest with the most correct answers wins a disposable camera.

The Price Is Right

Divide guests into teams of three to four players. Make an arrangement of basic baby items and challenge contestants to name the price of each item, without going over. Include items in a variety of price ranges, such as two diaper pins, a pacifier, a box of newborn diapers, a can of baby formula, a baby brush, a pair baby booties, a box of baby rice cereal, two baby undershirts, a collapsible umbrella stroller, a tub of baby wipes, a box of nursing pads, and two tubes of diaper rash ointment. The team with the most correct answers wins video rental certificates. Place all the baby items in the stroller for the guest of honor to take home.

8

Favors and Customs

As any child can tell you, a party is more fun when the guests tote home a goodie or two. Favors are a thoughtful gesture and a gracious way of thanking guests for sharing in the celebration. For some ethnic groups, party favors are an essential part of a shower, and guests would feel positively deprived if they were to go home without a small token. Everybody loves a parting gift no matter how small (which is something game show hosts have known for years).

Favors can be edible, whimsical, silly, practical, or just plain pretty. Use your imagination. There are favors to fit every theme and every party style imaginable—from handfuls of sweet Jordan almonds tied up with tulle (a bridal shower standard) to colorful leis for a Hawaiian-themed shower to rubber duckies for a baby shower.

Is the guest of honor a fanatic bridge player? Give guests packs of cards tied up with ribbon. Seed packets are a natural favor for a garden-themed shower. Is the mother-to-be a professional chef? Share a favorite recipe with guests, or give useful kitchen gadgets as favors. Beanbag animals or boxes of animal crackers are adorable favors for baby showers. Foil-wrapped choco-lates in beribboned boxes or cellophane bags are tasty tokens at any shower.

The favors need not be expensive, or they will eclipse the shower gifts. Just be sure to choose something that guests will really enjoy and really use. Forget about Cadillac-shaped ashtrays or kitschy figurines that will merely collect dust or be tossed in the trash later. Think twice about personalizing the favors with a sentiment such as "Jim and Alice's Spectacular Shower" or "Ginny's Baby Shower." While the guest of honor may get all choked up looking at bud vases engraved with her shower date for the next ten years, no one else will.

Where to Find Favors

Favors are available in party supply shops, craft stores, fabric stores, and some stationery and gift shops. You can also shop online or get great ideas from mail-order catalogs and party novelty suppliers. Don't be afraid to think off-beat. Visit a local magic shop for inexpensive magic tricks that guests will love trying at home. Dollar stores (shops that specialize in items priced under five dollars) and penny candy bins are gold mines when it comes to favors. Check out the local office supply shop for decorative magnets, picture frames, pencil holders, pocket calendars, and address books. Children's toy shops and the bath section of linen stores are great sources for treats like miniature Slinkys, Silly Putty, floating bathtub frogs, and fragrant soaps and lotions that are small enough to tuck into goody bags.

Buy loose candy or candy bars in bulk bags from a local wholesale club store. Use a personal computer and a high-quality parchment paper or vel-lum to print a personalized cover for candy bars. You can even scan a photo of the guest of honor and insert it onto the wrapper, along with a message like "Thanks for coming. Your presence made the party sweeter." Loose candy can be placed in little boxes or clear glassine bags decorated with sten-cils, buttons, or ribbons.

Craft and floral supply stores are invaluable resources for favor-making ideas and supplies. Ask the owner or manager to show you how to make a few basic styles. Many offer craft-making classes or pamphlets with step-by-step instructions.

Consider favors that double as centerpieces or place cards. Picture-frame favors work beautifully as place cards or menu holders. Purchase fragrant flowering bulbs such as hyacinth and daffodils and place them in terra-cotta pots that have been painted or sponged. Wrap the base of each pot with colorful florist-quality cellophane. Group five or six in a circle in the center of the table for a striking centerpiece, and give one to each guest as a shower favor. Check out the following suggested favors. Any of these items can also double as shower game prizes.

Bridal and Specialty Shower Favors

Address book

Aromatherapy oils or incense

Bath salts

Candlestick, votive candle holder, or scented candle

Splits of champagne

Chocolates: chocolate golf balls, custom-wrapped chocolate bar with couple's names, chocolate-covered spoon

Coasters

Compact or purse mirror

Cookie cutter or kitchen gadget

Create a mix of your favorite songs on a tape (or have professionally duplicated)

Crossword puzzle with pen (make your own using clues about a hobby such as shell collecting, or references to yourself or your family history)

Decorative fan

Decorative soaps tied up in tulle

Embroidered handkerchief

Flowering bulbs and instructions for planting

Fragrant sachet

Glass wine goblet

Heirloom family recipe, attached with ribbon to wooden spoon

Loofah sponge

Manicure set

Miniature photo album

Miniature glass vase with silk flower

Nail polish

Note cards or stationery

Phone card for free long-distance calls

Personal message rolled into a scroll

Place card holder in unusual shape (Adirondack chairs, houses, and so forth)

Refrigerator magnets

Pewter wine stopper

Picture frame

Regional food delicacy (maple syrup, jam, Maine blueberry jam, salsa, and so on)

Teacup and saucer

Scarf

Shower gel

Key ring

Specialty teas or coffees

Seed packet

Telephone pad and pencil

Gourmet jam, chili, fudge sauce, popcorn

Feather boa, Hawaiian lei, or tiara (for theme showers)

Small wooden birdhouse

Herb vinegar

Plume feather pen

Snow globe

Horoscopes

Gourmet candy apple

Biscotti wrapped in cellophane bags

Baby Shower Favors

Baby bottle filled with bubble bath

Baby bottle filled with candy, chocolate kisses, potpourri, popcorn, mints, jelly beans, or nuts

Baby powder tied with bow

Baby-size brush and comb for purse

Baby-size hand lotion or shampoo

Baby rattle

Baby teddy bear with pink or blue ribbon

Beanbag animal

Box of animal crackers

Box of chocolates tied with pink or blue ribbon

Box of crayons

Bud vase filled with baby's breath

Candy: Sugar Babies, Baby Ruth

Chocolate kisses

Cigars

Diaper pins attached to a card or hankie (They're great for nondiaper uses, too!)

Holiday ornament

Lace handkerchief tied with a pink or blue ribbon

Nosegay of dried flowers

Painted pink or blue terra-cotta pots filled with potting soil and a
small flowering bulb or plant

Pretty soaps

Pocket calendar with baby's due date circled

Potpourri in tulle bundle tied with pink or blue ribbon

Rubber ducky

Rubber stamps and ink pad

Scrapbook-making supplies

Single-use camera

Stuffed animal

Small picture frame

Slinky

Small toy

Silly Putty

Small photo album

Tape or CD with lullabies

Yo-yo

Shower Customs

Shower guests are expected to play traditional games or observe rituals. Many
of these rituals have been around for generations.

Perhaps the oldest ritual is the bow bouquet. When shower guests play the popular game of making a bow bouquet from the discarded gift ribbons, they are actually paying homage to an ancient courtship ritual. In many cultures, when the bride and groom were not allowed to see each other, they communicated through flowers. Young men were known to send their ladyloves bouquets of flowers specially chosen for the symbolic meanings of each bloom. Red roses meant passion, bluebells signified constancy, ivy signified fidelity, and marigold meant affection. If he wanted to declare his bashfulness, he sent peonies; if he wanted to announce secret love, he chose mimosas.

Ribbon and Bow Bouquet

Bridal showers often culminate with the hostess or maid of honor presenting to the bride a "bouquet" fashioned from the ribbons left over after the gifts are unwrapped. As each gift is opened, a previously appointed person takes the discarded trimmings and attaches them to a paper plate or floral bouquet form. The bouquet is later carried by the bride at the wedding rehearsal as she practices walking down the aisle.

Wishing Well

At many showers, guests are asked to bring a small gift (in addition to their shower gift) to place in a wishing well. These token gifts tend to be inexpensive household items such as a kitchen gadget, measuring cup, linen tea towel, scouring pad, or cookie cutter. For a baby shower, the wishing well gifts might include baby booties, a tube of diaper ointment, a plastic rattle, and so on. The presents are usually unwrapped and don't include a card. The shower hostess can make a homemade wishing well or buy or rent one at a party supply store.

Shower Umbrella

Ever notice how many party stores stock lacey umbrellas and paper plates or cups decorated with umbrella motifs? Since the umbrella is synonymous with showers and shelter, it's a fitting symbol at a baby, bridal, or specialty shower where friends gather to shower a guest of honor with gifts. Decorative umbrellas are available at craft, party, and bridal shops. Or shower hosts can make them themselves using any old umbrella from the hall closet and dressing it up with tulle, ribbons, streamers, or silk flowers.

Cake Charms

Here's a Southern custom that's truly charming. Wedding showers and bridesmaid luncheons in the South often include a cake-pulling ritual. The hostess ties tiny charms to ribbons that are inserted between the layers of the dessert cake. Each bridesmaid pulls out a ribbon and learns her fortune. The charms traditionally include an anchor (symbolizing travel or adventure); a ring (marriage); a horseshoe or four-leaf clover (good luck); a fleur-de-lis (love in full bloom); a thimble (the "old maid"); and a heart (love or the next person to marry).

Cake charms with attached ribbons are available through mail-order catalogs and anywhere shower accessories and favors are sold. They easily can be made by purchasing buttons or decorations in a fabric store and tying on the ribbons yourself.

Here Comes the Groom!

In the days before coed showers, the bridegroom was never invited to a shower. His job was to arrive a few minutes before the party concluded, greet the guests, and help the bride load the presents into the car. At some parties, that's still the case and guests view the arrival of the bridegroom as the official signal that the party is over.

The Morsel and the Old Maid

According to an old custom, any woman who eats the last piece of cake at a shower will remain on "old maid." (Ever notice that there's always a lone slice left on the plate?)

Tea for Thee

A shower tradition in some parts of the country is the formal tea-pouring ceremony. The honor of "pouring" (in some places it's quaintly known as "playing mother") usually falls on two close friends of the hostess. Actually, both tea and coffee are served. On one table or tray are a teapot, lemon slices, fresh mint, cream or milk, and a bowl with sugar cubes or granulated sugar. Another table holds a coffeepot, sugar, and cream pitcher. The first pourer holds the teacups in her left hand and pours the tea with her right. The second pourer holds the coffee cups in her left hand and pours the coffee with her right. This is a gracious custom based on the English afternoon tea tradition. It also makes serving hot beverages faster and easier.

Starting a New Shower Tradition

Every custom starts somewhere. Why not establish your own? Some families use a special punch bowl that is hauled out of the basement or attic for every special shower. Others use Grandma's special linens or silver. Consider these ideas for beginning a shower tradition.

Start a Shower Scrapbook If there are many babies or brides in the family, keep a separate page or two for each. For example, every time a family member has a baby shower, fill in a few pages for the guest of honor and their child. It's a great keepsake to bring out at family reunions years later.

Shower Host Plan Perhaps you'll want to start a tradition where the last person in the family (or circle of close friends) to receive a shower is the next in line to host one.

Special Shower Props Consider making or purchasing a wishing well and pass it along to the next person to host a shower. Or invest in a special linen tablecloth that is reserved for family milestone parties such as baby showers, wedding showers, birthdays, or anniversaries.

Priceless Treasures Give keepsake gifts such as a silver cup or silver platter that will last until the baby or bride has children of their own. These can be passed down from generation to generation.

Circle of Light Give each guest a candle and ask everyone to stand in a line or circle. Light the guest of honor's candle and have him or her light the candle of the next person, who in turn lights the next person's. This unity candle ceremony is very moving and makes for memorable pictures.

Make a Memory Quilt To commemorate the shower, ask each guest to bring a piece of fabric that can later be sewn into a quilt for the guest of honor. Imagine how comforting it might be to wrap yourself in a quilt that represents the love of your closest friends or family.

Appendix A: Resources

Gift Registry Sources

For information, contact these companies for referrals to online registries, or in-store gift registries in your area. Many of these online sites also feature helpful sections on planning a shower, including menus, themes, and decorating ideas.

China, Crystal, and Household Items

Bed Bath & Beyond	800-GO BEYOND	bedbathandbeyond.com
Fortunoff	800-367-8866	fortunoff.com
Lenox	800-423-8946	lenox.com
Linens 'n Things	800-568-8765	lnthings.com
Mikasa	800-833-4681	mikasa.com
Noritake	800-562-1991	noritake.com
Oneida Silversmith	800-877-6667	oneida.com
Pier 1 Imports	800-PIER-101	pier1.com
Pottery Barn	800-922-9934	potterybarn.com

Ross-Simons	800-556-7376	ross-simons.com
Swarovski Crystal	800-648-8210	swarovski.com
Tiffany & Company	800-526-0649	tiffany.com
Waterford Crystal	800-523-0009	waterford-usa.com

Appliances and Cooking Utensils

All-Clad Metalcrafters	800-255-2523	allclad.com
Calphalon	800-809-7267	calphalon.com
Farberware	516-794-3355	farberware.com
KitchenAid	800-541-6390	kitchenaid.com
Krups	800-526-5377	krups.com
Williams-Sonoma	800-840-2591	williams-sonoma.com

Stores and Mail-Order Catalogs

Eddie Bauer Home Collection	800-645-7467	eddiebauer.com
L. L. Bean	800-341-4341, ext. 38020	llbean.com
Bloomingdale's	800-888-2WED	bloomingdales.com
Bon-Ton	800-9-BON-TON	bonton.com
Crate and Barrel	800-967-6696	crateandbarrel.com
Dillard's Inc.	800-345-5273	dillards.com

Filene's	800-427-4337	filenesweddings.com
Fortunoff	800-367-8866	fortunoff.com
Hold Everything	800-840-3596	holdeverything.com
The Home Depot	800-553-3199	homedepot.com
JC Penney	800-JCP-GIFT	jcpenney.com
Macy's	800-92-BRIDES	macys.com
Marshall Field's	800-243-6436	marshallfields.com
Neiman Marcus	888-INCIRCLE	neimanmarcus.com
Pottery Barn	800-840-2843	potterybarn.com
Restoration Hardware	888-243-9720	restorationhardware.com
Service Merchandise	800-582-1960	servicemerchandise.com
Target	800-888-9333	target.com
Tiffany & Company	800-526-0649	tiffany.com
Tower Records	800-648-4844	towerrecords.com

Baby Gift Resources

American Girl (dolls)	800-845-0005	americangirl.com
Babies "R" Us	888-222-9787	babiesrus.com
Baby Bjorn	800-593-5522	babybjorn.com
Evenflo	800-233-5921	evenflo.com
Fisher Price	800-432-5437	fisherprice.com

Hearth Song	800-325-2502	hearthsong.com
Sears	800-407-4567	sears.com
Toys "R" Us	866-767-6943	toyrsus.com
Walmart	800-966-6546	walmart.com

Shower Invitations and Make-Your-Invitation Resources

American Stationery Company Inc.	800-822-2577	americanstationery.com
Anna Griffin Invitations	404-817-8170	annagriffin.com
Babies "R" Us	888-222-9787	babiesrus.com
Crane and Co.	800-268-2281	crane.com
Carlson Craft	800-292-9207	carlsoncraft.com
Dempsey & Carroll Stationery Engravers	800-444-4019	dempseyandcarroll.com
Embossed Graphics	800-325-1016	embossedgraphics.com
Idea Art	800-433-2278	ideaart.com
Internet Invitations	888-718-2523	internetinvitations.com
Paper Direct	800-443-2973	paperdirect.com
Paperstyle.com	770-667-6100	paperstyle.com
Papyrus	800-886-6700	papyrusonline.com
Renaissance Writings	800-246-8483	renaissancewritings.com
Rexcraft	800-635-3898	rexcraft.com

Resources for Shower Favors and Accessories

Beverly Clark Collection—800-888-6866; beverlyclark.com—Frames, glassware, bells, candy boxes, and more

Chandler's Candle Company—800-463-7143; chandlerscandle.com—Personalized candles and favors hand-decorated with dried flowers and hand-dipped in beeswax

Double T Ltd.—800-756-6184—Place-card favors featuring frames, chairs, teapots, music stands, and menu holders

Favors Favors—336-524-0028; favorsfavors.com—Cake boxes, fans, tote bags

First Impressions—angelbabies.com—Angel-theme favors

Florelle—800-768-7116; florelle.com—Wedding favor centerpieces and party-in-a-box packages

Godiva Chocolatier—800-9-GODIVA; godiva.com

Gratitude—800-914-4342; giftsofgratitude.com—Hand-finished boxes, note cards, and enclosures

Invitation Consultants—888-381-4400; invitationconsultants.com—Envelope seals, map cards, napkins, and much more

Lillian Vernon—800-545-5426; lillianvernon.com—Ornaments, party favors, inexpensive accessories, and personalized items

Little Favors—508-993-6800; littlefavors.com—Baby, wedding, special occasion party favors, cake tops, and piñatas

Magical Beginnings Butterfly Farm—888-639-9995; butterflyevents .com—Live Monarch butterflies to release

Martha by Mail—800-950-7130; marthabymail.com—Martha Stewart's glass-topped favor tins, dragées, Jordan Almonds, photograph stamps, favor bags and boxes, monogram stickers, ribbons, tulle, and finishing touches for making your own favors

Michaels, The Arts and Crafts Store—michaels.com—Dried flowers, crafts supplies, ribbons, favor boxes, and favors

Nuptial Bliss: The Wedding Phone Card—800-391-2642; nuptial bliss.com—Customized phone cards

Oriental Trading Company—800-228-2269; oriental.com—Crafts, stuffed animals, favors, toys, holiday/seasonal items, inspirational favors

Printed Candle Co.—800-605-0242; printedcandle.com—Decorative candles featuring dried flowers and other designs

Susan Morgan Elegant Cheesecakes—650-728-2248—Truly remarkable favors and specialty cakes and treats

Sweet Talk Promotions—800-50-FUDGE; sweettalkpromotions .com—Edible favors

Tree & Floral Beginnings—800-499-9580; plantamemory.com—Seeds, bulbs, and beeswax candles

Appendix B: Recipes

THE FOLLOWING RECIPES are tried-and-true shower fare. They comprise traditional favorites—including punches and main dishes—and have been contributed by food writers, chefs, and people who love to throw parties. Food editor Valerie Foster's Lime-Baked Chicken recipe is a winner for a shower on a chilly winter day; while her Tucson Turkey Salad is a light and refreshing entree for warm-weather entertaining. For an elegant ladies shower, consider Nancy Doyle's Veal and Water Chestnut Casserole. Also included is a recipe for a perennial shower classic, Chicken Salad with Green Grapes. These recipes were all chosen with ease of preparation in mind and many can be prepared ahead and/or frozen.

Beverages

Champagne Punch

2 cups sugar
2 cups lemon juice
4 cups canned pineapple cubes
1½ quarts water
1 bottle (750 ml) chilled white wine
2 25-ounce bottles chilled champagne
2 cups strawberries

175

In a large punch bowl, mix sugar and lemon juice. Add pineapple cubes, water, wine, and champagne. Add strawberries just before serving.

Makes about 24 servings

Classic Fruit Punch

If you've *ever* been to a baby or bridal shower, you've probably sipped this favorite.

    1 8-ounce can frozen orange juice
    1 8-ounce can frozen pineapple juice
    1 8-ounce can frozen lemonade
    Ice cubes or block of ice
    7–9 cups water
    1 quart ginger ale

Thaw juices and lemonade until slushy. Pour into a punch bowl over ice cubes or block of ice. Add water and ginger ale.

Makes 24 servings

Frozen Ice Ring

A pretty way to keep the punch chilled is with a prepared ice ring. Fill a doughnut-shaped ring gelatin mold with water. Add fresh strawberries, blueberries, or raspberries. If desired, add a few drops pink or yellow food coloring. Freeze until solid. Just before serving the punch, invert the ice mold and let it float on top of the punch.

Variation: Fill a ring mold with fruit sherbet and freeze until solid.

Mimosa Punch

>   2 quarts chilled orange juice
>   2 bottles chilled champagne
>   24 strawberries (optional)
>   Fresh mint leaves

Mix juice and champagne together. Place a strawberry in the bottom of each glass; or cut a small slice in each strawberry until nearly severed in half. Place one strawberry on the rim of each glass. Garnish with mint.

Makes 24 servings

Raspberry-Apple Punch

>   20 ounces frozen raspberries, thawed
>   12 cups chilled apple cider or apple juice
>   3 tablespoons lime juice

Puree raspberries in a blender. Strain through a sieve to remove seeds, if desired. Mix the berry puree, apple cider, and lime juice. Add ice cubes or a block of ice. (Or make another batch of punch and freeze some in an ice ring until solid.)

Makes 20 servings

Sangria for a Crowd

>   1 quart chilled orange juice
>   1 cup chilled lemon juice
>   ½ cup superfine sugar
>   1 gallon chilled red wine

½ cup brandy
1 cup chilled club soda
1 tray of ice cubes
2 oranges, sliced thin
2 lemons, sliced thin

Pour the orange juice and lemon juice into a punch bowl and add sugar. Stir well. Add red wine, brandy, club soda, ice cubes, and sliced fruit.

Makes 35 servings

Sparkling Party Punch

2 20-ounce cans crushed pineapple in its own juice
2 6-ounce cans frozen lemonade concentrate, thawed
1 28-ounce bottle club soda or ginger ale
3 tablespoons superfine sugar
1 25-ounce bottle champagne
½ gallon strawberry or raspberry sherbet (optional)
2 cups strawberries or raspberries

In a covered blender, blend the crushed pineapple until thick and slushy. Pour into punch bowl. Add cans of lemonade concentrate and club soda, sugar, and champagne. For a creamier version, add a half gallon of sherbet and stir. Float strawberries or raspberries on top. Add ice.

Makes about 24 servings

Dips

Blue Cheese Dip

2 cups sour cream

⅔ cup milk

8 ounces crumbled blue cheese

1 teaspoon hot pepper sauce

1 teaspoon Worcestershire sauce

Mix all ingredients together until smooth and blended. Chill thoroughly.

Makes 2 ½ cups

Easy Onion Dip

1 packet onion soup mix

2 cups sour cream

Blend the dried soup mix with the sour cream. Chill thoroughly.

Makes 2 cups

Florentine Dip

1 10-ounce package frozen chopped spinach

½ teaspoon dill

1 cup mayonnaise

1 cup sour cream or yogurt

½ cup chopped green onion or scallions

3 tablespoons chopped fresh parsley

Salt and freshly ground black pepper to taste

Thaw spinach in a colander to remove excess water. Mix together the spinach, dill, mayonnaise, sour cream, onion, and parsley until well-blended. Chill. Add salt and pepper to taste.

Makes 2 cups

Guacamole

2 medium avocados, cut into chunks
2 medium tomatoes, cut into chunks
1 medium onion, diced
2 tablespoons lemon juice
½ teaspoon hot pepper sauce

Blend all ingredients in a blender or food processor just until smooth. (Do not puree.)

Makes 2½ cups

Hot Glen Rock Crabmeat Dip

3 tablespoons milk
2 8-ounce packages cream cheese, softened
1 pound fresh lump crabmeat (or 2 8-ounce cans crabmeat)
2 tablespoons finely diced onion
1 to 2 tablespoons horseradish
1 teaspoon salt
Pepper or paprika to taste

Blend milk and cream cheese. Stir in the crabmeat. Add the onion, horse-radish, and salt. Spoon the mixture into a greased casserole dish. Sprinkle with pepper or paprika and bake at 375°F 15 to 20 minutes, until hot and bubbly. Serve warm. This is marvelous with crackers or French bread.

Makes 3 cups

Main Dishes and Side Dishes

Cheese Strata

Here's meatless recipe contributed by Jack Garceau, a cookbook writer and computer specialist from San Francisco. This dish is perfect for a brunch or light luncheon.

> 12 slices firm or day-old bread
> ½ cup butter
> 2 cups shredded cheddar cheese
> 2⅔ cups heavy cream
> 5 eggs
> ¾ teaspoon salt
> ¼ teaspoon dry mustard

Preheat oven to 350°F. Butter the bread. Place 6 slices in the bottom of a large casserole dish. Layer with cheese. Top with the remaining bread. Beat the cream, eggs, salt, and mustard together. Pour this mixture over the bread and cheese. Bake 45 minutes until strata is puffed and golden.

Variation: For a lower fat content, replace the heavy cream with milk and use 4 eggs instead of 5.

Makes 6–8 servings

Coleslaw for a Crowd

> 1 large green cabbage, shredded
> 1 large purple cabbage, shredded
> 1 large onion, diced
> 2 carrots, grated fine
> 2 cups sugar
> 2 cups red wine vinegar
> 1 cup vegetable oil
> 2 teaspoons celery seed
> 4 teaspoons prepared mustard
> Salt and freshly ground black pepper to taste

In a large bowl, toss cabbage, onion, and carrots with 1½ cups of the sugar. Set aside. In a small saucepan mix together remaining sugar, vinegar, oil, celery seed, and mustard. Bring the mixture to a boil, stirring constantly. Let it cool slightly. While mixture is still warm, pour it over the cabbage. Stir gently to coat thoroughly. Chill thoroughly before serving.

Makes 20 servings

Curried Chicken Salad

Chicken salad is a perennial favorite for shower fare because it's easy to make and easy to eat without balancing a knife and fork. This recipe adds the zingy spice of curry.

> 8 cups cooked diced or shredded chicken
> 2 cups slivered almonds
> 2 cups green grapes or raisins
> 2 cups sour cream (or plain yogurt, for lower fat content)
> 1½ cups high-quality mayonnaise

4 tablespoons lime juice

4–6 teaspoons sweet curry

1 teaspoon dried ginger

Fresh spinach or lettuce leaves (enough to line a serving platter)

Fresh parsley

Combine chicken, almonds, and grapes (or raisins). Set aside. Mix together sour cream, mayonnaise, lime juice, curry, and ginger. Toss with the chicken mixture. If the mixture is too dry, add more mayonnaise. Place spinach or lettuce leaves on large platter. Spoon the chicken mixture on top of leaves. Garnish with parsley.

Makes 6–8 servings

Meatless Lasagna

Jack Garceau makes this delicious vegetarian lasagna for friends.

2 pounds ricotta cheese

1 egg

1 package frozen, chopped spinach, cooked and drained

1 teaspoon sugar

½ teaspoon nutmeg

1 pound lasagna noodles

2 quarts spaghetti sauce

1 pound mozzarella cheese, grated or sliced

Preheat the oven to 325°F. Combine ricotta, egg, cooked spinach, sugar, and nutmeg; mix until smooth. Cook lasagna in four quarts boiling salted water for 6 minutes or until slightly underdone. Place ½ cup spaghetti sauce in the bottom of 13-by-9-inch baking pan. Add a layer of noodles, followed by a layer of ricotta, then a layer of mozzarella. Repeat twice. Top with the remaining sauce and mozzarella. Bake for 35 minutes, or until cheese is melted and browned.

Makes 8 servings

Nancy Doyle's Veal and Water Chestnut Casserole

This recipe is contributed by Nancy Doyle, a special events planner from Connecticut. She makes this elegant casserole for dinner parties—and guests never leave until they have the recipe! Don't omit the water chestnuts; their crunchy texture adds a nice contrast to the tender veal. Serve with hot rice or buttered noodles.

Variation: This recipe can also be prepared with beef cubes.

8 pounds veal, cut into 1-inch cubes
2 cups butter
4 medium onions, minced
4 cloves garlic, peeled and crushed
2 tablespoons salt, or to taste
2 teaspoons freshly ground black pepper
3–4 pounds mushrooms, sliced thin
4 cups bouillon
4 bay leaves
8 6-ounce cans water chestnuts, drained and sliced
8 cups cream
1 cup cognac
Dash of nutmeg
¾ cup chopped parsley

Preheat the oven to 375°F. In a large sauté pan, sauté the veal in the butter until browned. Add onions and garlic and cook 5 minutes more. Season with salt and pepper. Remove the meat and transfer it to a large covered casserole dish. Add mushrooms to the onion and garlic mixture and sauté a few minutes more. Add this mixture to the meat in casserole dish. Deglaze the sauté pan with bouillon, scraping up the browned bits. Add bouillon and browned bits to the meat. Add bay leaves and sliced water chestnuts to the casserole dish. Cover and bake for 1½ hours. Add cream and stir. Remove the cover and cook 15 minutes. Add cognac and nutmeg and stir. Cook an additional 10 minutes, until the mixture is very hot and the sauce has thickened. Sprinkle with parsley. Serve over hot rice or buttered noodles.

Makes 24–28 servings

The recipes for Lime-Baked Chicken, Roasted Asparagus with Parmesan, Tortellini Salad, and Tucson Turkey Salad were contributed by Valerie Foster, an award-winning food writer and features editor of *The Advocate* newspaper in Stamford, Connecticut, and the *Greenwich Time* newspaper in Greenwich, Connecticut

Valerie Foster's Lime-Baked Chicken

1 cup Dijon mustard
½ cup lime juice
6 tablespoons chicken bouillon granules
4 teaspoons crushed dried tarragon leaves
4 teaspoons crushed dried rosemary leaves
8 pounds skinless boneless chicken breasts
4 tablespoons diced fresh parsley leaves
Salt and freshly ground black pepper to taste
4 limes, sliced thin

Preheat the oven to 325°F. Mix together mustard, lime juice, bouillon granules, tarragon, and rosemary. Rub mixture on chicken breasts. Place them in a baking dish. Sprinkle with parsley and salt and pepper to taste. Top with lime slices. Bake 40 minutes (uncovered) or until chicken is tender.

Makes 24 servings

Valerie Foster's Roasted Asparagus with Parmesan

8 pounds fresh, thick asparagus
8 tablespoons extra-virgin olive oil
Kosher salt to taste
½ pound Parmigiana-Reggiano cheese, thinly shaved

Preheat oven to 500°F. Snap off woody ends of each asparagus spear. Cut each spear—on the diagonal—into 4 pieces. Toss with olive oil. Place asparagus in 2 15-by-10-by-1-inch jelly roll pans. Sprinkle lightly with Kosher salt. Bake 10 to 15 minutes, depending on the thickness of the spears, until crisp-tender, turning at least 4 times. Transfer the asparagus to a serving platter. Sprinkle the shaved cheese over the top of the asparagus. Serve immediately or at room temperature.

Makes 24 servings

Valerie Foster's Tortellini Salad

Vinaigrette:

12 tablespoons red wine vinegar
6 tablespoons lemon juice
12 teaspoons Dijon mustard
1 cup fresh dill
6 cups chopped parsley leaves

6 garlic cloves, peeled

1¼ cups extra-virgin olive oil

Salt and pepper to taste

Salad:

5 pounds cheese tortellini

1 pound prosciutto, slivered

2 pounds small grape tomatoes (or cherry tomatoes, cut in half)

2 cups pitted diced Kalamata olives

1½ cups diced scallions, green parts included

Romaine lettuce leaves (enough to line a large serving platter)

Place vinegar, lemon juice, mustard, dill, parsley, and garlic in the work bowl of a food processor. Pulse until garlic is pulverized and all ingredients are well mixed. Add olive oil, a little at a time, through a feed tube, until incorporated with ingredients. Add salt and pepper to taste.

Meanwhile, cook the tortellini in boiling salted water until done. Immediately drain the tortellini and add the vinaigrette. Add all remaining ingredients except the lettuce leaves. Mix well to coat the tortellini thoroughly.

Line a platter with the romaine leaves. Top with the tortellini mixture. Either serve salad immediately or at room temperature. If the salad is refrigerated, be sure to bring it to room temperature before serving.

Makes 24 servings

Valerie Foster's Tucson Turkey Salad

2 pounds sour cream

4 tablespoons lemon juice

2 teaspoons ground cumin

¼ teaspoon Tabasco sauce

Iceberg lettuce leaves

3 pounds smoked turkey breast, cut into cubes

3 pounds cheddar cheese, cubed

5 Granny Smith apples, cored, diced, and tossed with 2 tablespoons
  lemon juice

4 cups sliced celery

4 cups diced jicama

1 cup walnut pieces, toasted in 350°F oven for 5 minutes

To make the dressing:

In a medium bowl, combine the sour cream, lemon juice, cumin, and Tabasco sauce. Cover and chill 1 hour.

To make the salad:

Place lettuce leaves on serving platter. Arrange turkey, cheese, apples, celery, and jicama over lettuce. Sprinkle with walnuts. Serve the dressing on the side.

Makes 24 servings

Desserts

Blueberry Streusel Coffee Cake

This is the ultimate coffee cake—fine crumbed; easy to cut into squares; and absolutely delicious for brunch, luncheon dessert, or afternoon tea.

Try it with raisins or nuts instead of blueberries. Cake flour gives the cake a lighter texture, but you can make it with all-purpose flour, too.

Cake:

> 2 cups plus 4 tablespoons cake flour (or substitute 2 cups sifted all-purpose flour)
> 2¼ teaspoons double-acting baking powder
> ¾ cup sugar
> ¾ teaspoon salt
> 2 eggs, well-beaten
> ½ cup milk
> ½ cup salad oil
> 1 cup blueberries (It's fine to use frozen solid blueberries.)

Streusel topping:

> ⅔ cup packed brown sugar
> 2 tablespoons white sugar
> 6 tablespoons all-purpose flour
> 1 teaspoon cinnamon
> 5 tablespoons butter or margarine
> 1 teaspoon vanilla

To make the cake batter:

Preheat the oven to 400°F. Mix the flour, baking powder, sugar, and salt. Set aside. Combine eggs, milk, and oil, and add to the dry ingredients until just blended. Don't overbeat. Pour batter into a greased and floured 9-inch-square pan. Scatter blueberries over the top.

To make the streusel:

Combine the sugars, flour, cinnamon, butter, and vanilla. Spoon the topping evenly over the batter. Bake 30–35 minutes until a cake tester inserted into the center comes out clean. Let cake cool and then cut into squares.

Makes 9 servings

Father Tony's Buttermilk-Glazed Carrot Cake

This recipe, courtesy of Reverend Tony Serio (formerly of St. Catherine's Church in Glen Rock, New Jersey) is incredibly moist; and the not-too-sweet buttermilk glaze is worth the effort.

Cake:

    2 cups all-purpose flour
    1 teaspoon baking soda
    ½ teaspoon salt
    1½ cups sugar
    3 eggs
    ¾ cup buttermilk
    ½ cup salad oil (corn or vegetable, but *not* olive oil)
    2 teaspoons vanilla
    8½ ounces crushed pineapple
    2 cups finely grated carrot
    1 cup coarsely chopped walnuts
    1 cup flaked coconut

Buttermilk glaze:

    ⅔ cup sugar
    ¼ teaspoon baking soda

⅓ cup buttermilk

2 tablespoons light corn syrup

½ teaspoon vanilla

To make the cake:

Preheat the oven to 350°F. Stir together the flour, baking soda, salt, and sugar. Set aside. Lightly beat together the eggs, buttermilk, oil, and vanilla; add the dry ingredients and stir until blended. Fold in the pineapple, carrots, nuts, and coconut. Pour into a greased and floured 9-by-13-inch pan. Bake 45 minutes, or until the center springs back when lightly touched. Remove from the oven and gently prick the cake's surface with the tines of a fork. Let the cake cool while preparing glaze.

To make the glaze:

Place the sugar, baking soda, buttermilk, and corn syrup in a medium saucepan. Bring to a boil over medium heat, stirring constantly. Boil gently for 5 minutes, remove from heat, and stir in the vanilla. Let cool 5 minutes, then slowly pour the glaze over top of the cake. Chill the cake for at least 1 hour before serving.

Makes 8–10 servings

Miniature Cheesecakes

12 vanilla wafers (or similar-size chocolate chip cookies)

2 8-ounce packages cream cheese, slightly softened

1 cup sugar

2 eggs

1 teaspoon vanilla or almond extract

1 12-ounce can blueberry or cherry pie filling

Preheat the oven to 325°F. Line muffin tins with paper or foil cupcake liners. Drop one vanilla wafer (or chocolate chip cookie) into each liner. On medium speed, beat cream cheese with sugar until fluffy. Add eggs one at a time. Add vanilla extract, and blend thoroughly. Do not overbeat.

Spoon sweetened cream cheese mixture over wafers, filling each about three-quarters full. Bake for 25 minutes. Chill thoroughly. Just before serving, spoon 1 or 2 tablespoons of pie filling over each cheesecake.

Makes 12 servings

Shower Flowerpot

Astound guests by serving dessert straight from the flowerpot centerpiece! In this recipe, crushed chocolate cookies make for realistic-looking dirt that tops a rich chocolate mousse base. You'll need a clean, new flowerpot lined with aluminum foil, and four or five real or artificial flowers on long stems for "planting" in the pot. (For a speedier version, make two packages of instant pudding, instead of mousse.) Spoon it out each serving using a clean, new garden trowel.

Because of the risk of salmonella, be sure to use only the freshest eggs, purchased from a grocer whose stock is replenished frequently. If in doubt, substitute prepared chocolate pudding for the mousse mixture.

Terra-cotta or plastic flowerpot, 8-inch diameter
1 pound chocolate sandwich cookies, crushed
1½ cups heavy cream, whipped
Candy worms (optional)

Mousse filling:

1½ pounds semisweet chocolate chips
½ cup prepared espresso
4 egg yolks

2½ cups heavy cream
¼ cup sugar
8 egg whites

Line the flowerpot with aluminum foil (be sure to cover the hole at the bottom of the pot). Place the cookies in a Ziploc plastic bag and crush using a rolling pin. Pour about a third of the cookie crumbs into the bottom of the pot. Set the rest aside along with the whipped cream.

Melt chocolate chips in a microwave or double boiler. Stir in the espresso and let the mixture cool to room temperature. Add egg yolks one at a time, mixing well after each addition. Whip the cream until it is thickened; add sugar gradually and beat it until it is stiff. In a separate bowl, beat egg whites until stiff. Fold egg whites into the cream mixture. Gently fold in the chocolate one third at a time. Chill at least 1 hour

To assemble: Spoon in a layer of the chocolate mousse; followed by a layer of whipped cream and a layer of cookie crumbs. Repeat the layering. Sprinkle the remaining crumbs over the top. Chill for several hours. Before serving, insert the flowers into the pot and add candy worms, if desired.

(Note: If you are using the flowerpot as a centerpiece, place it on the table no more than 30 minutes before serving. For food safety reasons, the mousse and cream should be refrigerated until then.)

Makes 8–10 servings

Walnut Squares

Imagine a cross between butterscotch brownies and pecan pie. These are just that chewy and yummy.

1 egg
1 cup packed brown sugar

1 teaspoon vanilla
½ cup flour
¼ teaspoon baking soda
¼ teaspoon salt
1 cup chopped walnuts

Preheat oven to 350°F. Mix together the egg, brown sugar, and vanilla. Stir in flour, baking soda, and salt. Add walnuts and stir. Pour into a greased 8-inch-square pan. Bake for 18–20 minutes until browned and set.

Makes 16 squares

Appendix C: Bridal Gift Registry

TOO MANY TOASTERS! It's not unusual for brides to receive duplicate gifts during the rounds of prewedding parties and showers. That can mean four cappuccino makers and enough electric blankets to melt the polar ice caps. To avoid the problem of duplications and provide a convenience for shower guests, encourage the bride to register her choices through a bridal registry.

Registering simply means recording preferences (and quantities) in a variety of categories, along with the wedding date, color, and pattern choices and where the gifts may be sent. The store, or online registry service, keeps this information on file for guests to consult. As a result, the bride and groom receive the gifts they love and will really use, and guests appreciate not having to second-guess the couple's wish list.

When planning a bridal shower, find out where the bride is registered. Guests will definitely want to know. While it's considered crass to list registry information on a wedding invitation, it's perfectly appropriate (and encouraged!) to include where the bride is registered on a shower invitation. That's because a shower is a less formal, more intimate social occasion and gift giving is the whole reason for the party in the first place!

If you're hosting a shower, you're bound to receive calls from guests asking for gift ideas for the couple. It's a good idea to compile a list for easy reference. You might want to copy and distribute the list to friends and loved ones. Be sure to sit down with the bride—or, even better, the bride *and* the

Dear Friends,

Everyone has been asking me for shower gift ideas for Elvis and Priscilla! I know that your presence at the shower will be a present in itself, but here are a few ideas to help you make a choice. Elvis and Priscilla are registered at:

Hunk a Burnin' Love Fireplace Emporium

Blue Suede Shoes Boutique

Both stores have branches in Nashville and Las Vegas, but you can call for the registry lists and order gifts over the phone.

They've also shared their personal wish list with me. They would appreciate:

- A gift certificate for dinner for two at The Barbecue Pit in Nashville

- Lumber to build the garden trellis Priscilla's been longing for

- Live plants and flowering bulbs for their garden

- Gift certificates to Michael's craft store (Elvis always needs glitter and sequins!)

- Sheets, towels, and pillowcases in a leopard print design

- Contributions to their favorite charity for children

The decorating scheme for their new home is country casual. The colors they favor are black and red for the bathrooms, animal prints for the bedroom, and yellow and white for the kitchen. I'm looking for someone to split the cost of an outdoor grill for them. Anyone interested? See you all at the shower!

Karen Hartland

Matron of Honor

groom—and ask about color preferences, decorating scheme, and any special items they would love or could really use.

If the shower is a surprise, consult with the bride's and groom's parents, roommates, siblings, or members of the bridal party. Remember that it's thoughtful to include gifts in a wide price range.

Bridal Gift Ideas/Registry

A good place for the bride to begin is by prioritizing these general categories:

Bed and bath items

Cookware and bakeware

Kitchen gadgets and accessories

Kitchen appliances

Formal and casual dinnerware

Flatware

Fine china place settings

Silverware

Barware and glassware

Serving accessories

Fine crystal

Table linens

Personal-care products

Home furnishings

Patio, garden, and landscape items

Home electronics

Paint, lumber, and home-decorating supplies

Hardware and tools

Contributions to charity, scholarship fund, or mortgage fund

Formal Dinnerware

☐ Dinner plates

☐ Salad or dessert plates

☐ Teacups and saucers

☐ Soup plates

☐ Teapot

☐ Coffeepot

☐ Covered vegetable dish

☐ Casserole dish

☐ Platters

☐ Serving bowls

☐ Gravy boat

☐ Salt and pepper shakers

Everyday (Casual) Dinnerware

- ☐ Dinner plates
- ☐ Salad or dessert plates
- ☐ Teacups and saucers
- ☐ Soup plates
- ☐ Cereal bowls
- ☐ Ice cream/sherbet bowls
- ☐ Teapot
- ☐ Coffeepot
- ☐ Covered vegetable dish
- ☐ Casserole dish
- ☐ Platters
- ☐ Serving bowls
- ☐ Gravy boat
- ☐ Salt and pepper shakers

Formal Flatware: Silver and/or Silver-Plated Place Settings

- ☐ Knife
- ☐ Fork

- ☐ Salad fork

- ☐ Teaspoon

- ☐ Cream soup spoon

- ☐ Iced tea or sundae spoon

- ☐ Tablespoon

- ☐ Pierced tablespoon

- ☐ Butter knife

- ☐ Berry spoon

- ☐ Cold meat fork

- ☐ Gravy boat

- ☐ Well and tree platter

- ☐ Pie or cake server

- ☐ Sugar spoon

- ☐ Silver chest

- ☐ Candlesticks

- ☐ Salad tongs or salad servers

- ☐ Serving spoons

- ☐ Serving forks

- ☐ Pickle/lemon fork

- ☐ Cheese knife

Everyday (Casual) Flatware: Silver and/or Silver-Plated Place Settings

☐ Knife

☐ Fork

☐ Dessert fork

☐ Teaspoon

☐ Tablespoon or dessert spoon

☐ Butter knife

☐ Meat fork

☐ Gravy boat or ladle

☐ Pie or cake server

☐ Sugar spoon

☐ Salad tongs

☐ Serving spoons

☐ Serving forks

☐ Cheese knife

☐ Spaghetti tongs

Fine Crystal

☐ Champagne glasses (flute, tulip, or sherbet-shaped)

☐ Cordial or liqueur glasses

☐ Water goblets

☐ Tumblers

☐ Red wine glasses

☐ White wine glasses

☐ Brandy snifters

☐ Pitcher

☐ Crystal ice bucket

☐ Crystal decanter

☐ Crystal vase

☐ Crystal sugar and creamer

☐ Crystal candy dish

☐ Crystal serving bowl

Cookware

☐ Omelet pan

☐ Skillet or fry pan (assorted sizes)

☐ Wok

☐ Dutch oven

☐ Stockpot

☐ Saucepan (1-quart, 4-quart)

☐ Shallow roasting pan

☐ Vegetable steamer basket

☐ Sauté pan (3-quart, 5-quart, or 7-quart)

☐ Roasting/broiling rack

☐ Large covered roasting pan

☐ Double boiler

☐ Tongs

☐ Large slotted spoon

☐ Large serving fork

☐ Meat thermometer

☐ Ladle

☐ Potato masher

☐ Grater

Glasses and Barware

☐ On-the-rocks glasses

☐ Juice glasses (4-ounce or 8-ounce)

☐ Champagne glasses

☐ Water goblets (10-ounce)

☐ Wineglasses (all-purpose)

☐ Highball glasses

☐ Shot glasses

☐ Old-fashioned glasses

☐ Beer or pilsner glasses

☐ Iced Tea or Tumbler glasses (12-ounce)

☐ Margarita glasses

☐ Martini glasses

☐ Wine rack

☐ Cocktail shaker

☐ Vacuum seal caps

☐ Decorative wine stoppers

☐ Bar utensils

☐ Pitcher

☐ Coasters

☐ Cocktail napkins

☐ Ice bucket and tongs

Bakeware

☐ Cake pans (round)

☐ Cake pans (8-inch-square)

☐ Cake pans (13-by-9-inch)

☐ Muffin pans

☐ Cookie sheets

☐ Cookie rack

- ☐ Jelly roll pan

- ☐ Madeleine pans

- ☐ Popover pans

- ☐ Corn-bread stick pans

- ☐ Loaf pan

- ☐ Bundt pan

- ☐ Tube pan

- ☐ Measuring cups

- ☐ Measuring spoons

- ☐ Oven mitts

- ☐ Pot holders

- ☐ Cookbook holder

- ☐ Sifter

- ☐ Pie pans

- ☐ Parchment paper

- ☐ Muffin, cupcake papers

- ☐ Rolling pin

- ☐ Pie weights

- ☐ Miniature tart pans

- ☐ Mixing bowls

☐ Spatulas

☐ Wooden spoons

☐ Baking stone (for making pizza and bread)

Kitchen Items and Serving Accessories

☐ Canisters

☐ Spice rack

☐ Coffee grinder

☐ Food storage containers

☐ Shelf liners

☐ Dish drainer

☐ Blender

☐ Cookie jar

☐ Dishcloths and towels

☐ Oven mitts and pot holders

☐ Grater

☐ Lemon squeezer

☐ Egg separator

☐ Cookbooks and rack

☐ Lazy Susan

☐ Meat thermometer

☐ Candy thermometer

☐ Rack for hanging pots or utensils

☐ Timer

☐ Trivets

☐ Handmixer

☐ Manual can opener

☐ Bottle opener

☐ Kitchen mixer

☐ Place mats

☐ Kitchen shears

☐ Platters

☐ Carving fork

☐ Salad spinner

☐ Eggbeater

☐ Pastry blender

☐ Knives

— Paring

— Boning

— Cleaver

— Bread (serrated)

— Utility knife

— Sharpening steel

___ Chef's knife

___ Steak knives

☐ Colander

☐ Pasta maker

☐ Balloon whisk

☐ Kitchen scale

☐ Platters

☐ Bowls

☐ Covered casserole dishes

☐ Chafing dish

☐ Compote dish

☐ Trifle bowl

☐ Trivets

☐ Cutting board

☐ Tray

☐ Extra serving spoons

☐ Bread basket

☐ Salad bowl

☐ Canning jars and accessories

☐ Pie or cake server

☐ Gravy boat and ladle

Kitchen and Home Electric Appliances

- ☐ Coffeemaker
- ☐ Electric can opener
- ☐ Blender
- ☐ Electric mixer
- ☐ Toaster
- ☐ Toaster oven
- ☐ Bread maker
- ☐ Microwave oven
- ☐ Convection oven
- ☐ Food processor
- ☐ Cappuccino or espresso maker
- ☐ Electric frying pan
- ☐ Waffle iron
- ☐ Crepe maker
- ☐ Juicer
- ☐ Electric steamer
- ☐ Warming tray
- ☐ Crock-Pot
- ☐ Egg poacher
- ☐ Yogurt maker

- ☐ Pressure cooker
- ☐ Popcorn maker
- ☐ Smoke detector
- ☐ Iron and ironing board
- ☐ Vacuum cleaner
- ☐ Rug cleaner
- ☐ Flashlights
- ☐ Telephone
- ☐ Answering machine
- ☐ Television
- ☐ Fire extinguisher
- ☐ Stereo equipment
- ☐ VCR
- ☐ DVD player
- ☐ Digital camera
- ☐ Videocamera
- ☐ Camera
- ☐ Sewing machine
- ☐ Computer
- ☐ Printer

☐ Scanner

☐ Fax machine

☐ Palm pilot

☐ Portable phone

Bed and Bath Items

Find out which size linens and bedding the couple will need: king, queen, double, full, or twin.

Linens and bedroom items:

☐ Fitted and flat sheets

☐ Pillowcases

☐ Pillow shams

☐ Quilts

☐ Duvet and cover

☐ Mattress pads

☐ Pillows (king or standard)

☐ Dust ruffle (bedskirt)

☐ Bedspread

☐ Comforter

☐ Patchwork quilt

☐ Thermal blanket

☐ Electric blanket

☐ Matching curtains

☐ Valance or shade

☐ Bedside table and cover

☐ Accessories

    ___ Lamp

    ___ Framed prints

    ___ Rug or carpeting

    ___ Chair pads

☐ Closet organizers

☐ Scented drawer liners

☐ Drawer organizers

Table Linens

Find out the couple's preferred tablecloth shape (round, square, rectangle, or oval) and what size table they have.

☐ Tablecloths

☐ Runners

☐ Dinner napkins

☐ Luncheon napkins

☐ Cocktail napkins

☐ Napkin rings

☐ Place mats

Bath Linens and Accessories

☐ Shower curtain

☐ Shower rings

☐ Curtain liner

☐ Bath mat

☐ Bath sheet

☐ Bath towels

☐ Hand towels

☐ Washcloths

☐ Guest towels

☐ Bathroom window treatments

☐ Bathroom rug

☐ Scale

☐ Clothes hamper

☐ Soap dish

☐ Toothbrush holder

☐ Tissue box cover

☐ Wastebasket

☐ Towel rack

☐ Closet organizers

☐ Framed decorative prints

Home Furnishings and Accessories

For big-ticket items such as furniture or entertainment centers, consider sharing the cost with other shower guests. A group gift makes shopping easier for everyone, and the couple will be thrilled to receive something they might have had to save a long time for.

☐ Sofa or loveseat

☐ Rugs

☐ Curtains

☐ Cedar chest

☐ Tray tables

☐ Side chair

☐ Recliner

☐ Coffee table or cocktail table

☐ Lamps

☐ Mirror

☐ Paintings or decorative art

☐ Fireplace set

☐ Fans

☐ Clock

- ☐ Console

- ☐ End tables

- ☐ Entertainment center

- ☐ Armoire

- ☐ Bar unit

- ☐ Armchair

- ☐ Secretary or desk

- ☐ Bookcases

- ☐ Storage units

- ☐ Occasional tables

- ☐ Blanket/storage chest

- ☐ Hope chest

- ☐ Cedar chest

- ☐ Chest of drawers

- ☐ Bedroom set

- ☐ Dining room table and chairs

- ☐ China cupboard or sideboard

- ☐ Chandelier

- ☐ Computer desk

- ☐ Wall unit

- ☐ Exercise or sporting equipment

- ☐ Sleeper sofa

- ☐ Decorative accessories

Exterior House and Garden Items

- ☐ Patio furniture

- ☐ Outdoor grill

- ☐ Power tools

- ☐ Hardware and tools

- ☐ Picnic table and chairs

- ☐ Outdoor benches

- ☐ Chaise lounge

- ☐ Umbrella

- ☐ Garage accessories

- ☐ Outdoor storage unit

- ☐ Sawhorse

- ☐ Paint or lumber for home projects

- ☐ Trellis or arbor

- ☐ Seeds, trees, plant material

- ☐ Mulch

- ☐ Shrubs

- ☐ Gutters

Appendix D: Baby Gift Registry

BRIDES TEND TO BE savvy about using a gift registry to record their gift preferences; after all, wedding gift registries have been around for generations. Baby gift registries are not as well known, but they can be just as useful! Using a registry makes it easier for guests to select gifts that truly will be appreciated.

If you're hosting a shower, be sure to include on the invitation where the guest of honor is registered. It's easy to find lists of baby care and clothing items in magazines for expectant mothers or online. Many toy and juvenile furniture stores also have computerized registry services or kiosks in the store. Take advantage of these free services.

If you prefer to write a note to guests, consider the format shown here.

> Dear Friends,
>
> Everyone has been asking me for baby shower gift ideas for Martha and George. I know your presence at the shower will be a present in itself, but here are a few ideas to help you make a choice. Martha is registered at:
>
> Rubber Ducky Boutique
>
> Juvenile Jungle

Both stores have branches in the Midwest and Northeast, but you can call for the registry lists and order gifts over the phone.

George and Martha have also shared their personal wish list with me. They would appreciate:

* A chest of drawers for the baby's clothes and diapers

* Beatrix Potter–themed crib bumpers, blanket, and crib sheets

* The adorable bunny lamp at Child World on Market Street in Castleton

* A Jenny Lind–style crib in white or brown

* One of those collapsible strollers that fits easily in the car

* Cloth diapers or a diaper service

* Any baby clothes at all! They need everything!

They aren't planning to dress the baby in only pink or blue, so any colors are fine. I know they both love yellow and hate red. I'm looking for a few people to split the cost of a new washer for them, so let me know if you're interested. See you all at the shower!

Diana Cutaia
Shower Hostess

Layette Items and Baby Basics

Find out if the new parents plan to use cloth or disposable diapers, or a diaper service. Newborns use up to six dozen diapers a week!

- ☐ Diapers
- ☐ Diaper service
- ☐ Cloth diapers
- ☐ Disposable diapers
- ☐ 4–6 waterproof pants
- ☐ 6–8 safety pins to use with cloth diapers
- ☐ 4–6 diaper covers

Baby Care Items

- ☐ Diaper rash cream
- ☐ Diaper pail
- ☐ Diaper pail liners
- ☐ Diaper pail disinfectant
- ☐ Baby powder (cornstarch)
- ☐ Baby bath
- ☐ Tweezers
- ☐ Nasal aspirator
- ☐ Plastic bath tub
- ☐ 6–8 baby washcloths
- ☐ 3–4 hooded bath towels
- ☐ Baby soap and shampoo

- ☐ Baby nail clippers

- ☐ Medicine spoon or dropper

- ☐ Thermometer

- ☐ Pacifier thermometer

- ☐ Baby wipes

- ☐ Lotion

- ☐ Brush and comb

- ☐ Vaporizer or humidifier

- ☐ Baby-sitter wipe-off board (for writing important phone numbers and instructions)

- ☐ First-aid kit

- ☐ Infant and baby care book

Accessories and Nursery Furniture

- ☐ Crib

- ☐ Bassinet (fits newborn to two months only)

- ☐ Crib bumpers

- ☐ Mattress

- ☐ Changing table

- ☐ Chest of drawers

- ☐ Nursery room curtains or shades

- ☐ Nursery room rug
- ☐ Rocking chair
- ☐ Infant car seat
- ☐ Stroller or baby carriage
- ☐ Collapsible stroller for travel
- ☐ High chair
- ☐ Plastic floor protector (for placing under high chair)
- ☐ Playpen
- ☐ Portable travel crib
- ☐ Infant carrier
- ☐ Mobile
- ☐ Wall decorations
- ☐ Lamp
- ☐ Decorative accessories
- ☐ Stuffed animals
- ☐ Baby monitor
- ☐ "Baby on Board" sign for car
- ☐ Glare screen for car
- ☐ Clothing hooks
- ☐ Decorative shelves

☐ Armoire

☐ Music box

☐ Mirror

☐ Snugly or baby backpack

☐ Diaper bag

Bedding Items

☐ Mattress pad

☐ 2–3 waterproof mattress covers

☐ 1–2 washable changing table pads

☐ 6–8 crib sheets

☐ 6–8 bassinet sheets

☐ 5–6 receiving blankets

☐ 2–3 full-size crib blankets

Baby Clothes

For newborn:

☐ Outfit to bring baby home from hospital

☐ Sweater or heavy bunting (depending on time of year)

☐ Cap (brimmed sun bonnet or woolen cap, depending on season)

☐ 6–8 snap-in-front undershirts

☐ 6–8 footed creepers

- ☐ 2–3 open-footed creepers

- ☐ 2–3 pull-on pants

- ☐ 6–8 sleep gowns

- ☐ 3–4 pairs booties

- ☐ 4–6 cloth diapers (for use as burp cloths)

- ☐ 6–8 feeding bibs

For babies 3 months and older:

- ☐ 4–6 long sleeve shirts

- ☐ 4–6 short sleeve shirts

- ☐ 6–8 one-piece undershirts (snap between legs)

- ☐ 2–3 sweaters (at least one should be an easy to put on cardigan)

- ☐ 4–6 pairs snug stretchy socks or booties

- ☐ Baby cap

- ☐ 4–6 pairs of pants

- ☐ 2 dressy outfits

- ☐ Tights or socks

Miscellaneous

Find out if the new mom intends to breast-feed or bottle feed.

- ☐ Breast pump

- ☐ Nursing bras

- ☐ Nursing shirts

- ☐ Nursing nightgowns

- ☐ Bottles and nipples (4-ounce and 8-ounce sizes)

- ☐ Bottle cleaning brush

- ☐ Formula

- ☐ Can opener

- ☐ Fully stocked travel diaper bag for the car, office, or travel

- ☐ Rattle

- ☐ Pacifier

- ☐ Powdered baby formula

- ☐ Book on infant care

- ☐ Pacifier thermometer (It takes the temperature while resting in baby's mouth!)

- ☐ Baby knife, fork, and spoon

- ☐ Baby keepsake porcelain plate

- ☐ Baby plastic plate (with suction bottom for attaching to table)

- ☐ Smoke detector for baby's room

- ☐ Film, camera, and batteries

- ☐ Grandma's brag book for photographs

Extremely Thoughtful Gifts

- ☐ A week's worth of nutritious dinners for the parents to enjoy after the baby comes home

- ☐ An elastic-waist skirt, stretchy leggings, and oversize tunic for the postpartum mom

- ☐ Handwritten coupons for baby-sitting, housecleaning, food delivery, or help with errands

- ☐ Basket with videotapes, popcorn, bottle of wine, and cheese and crackers for new parents

- ☐ Gift certificate for manicure and pedicure for mom

- ☐ Basket full of baby lotion, baby oil, shampoo, and washcloths

- ☐ Basket full of baby food in jars, baby rice, bottles, plastic bowls, spoons, bib

- ☐ Basket full of spa treatments for mom

- ☐ Basket with disposable camera or film, prepaid photo mailers, and baby scrapbook

Index